T. D.
JAKES

T. D.
JAKES

Sam Wellman

CHELSEA HOUSE PUBLISHERS
Philadelphia

Chelsea House Publishers

Editor in Chief	Stephen Reginald
Production Manager	Pamela Loos
Art Director	Sara Davis
Director of Photography	Judy L. Hasday
Managing Editor	James D. Gallagher

Staff for T. D. JAKES

Associate Art Director	Takeshi Takahashi
Editorial Assistant	Robert Quinn
Picture Researcher	Sandy Jones
Designer	Keith Trego

Cover Photo: Philadelphia Inquirer/John Costello

The Chelsea House World Wide Web address is
http://www.chelseahouse.com

First Printing

1 3 5 7 9 8 6 4 2

Wellman, Sam.
   T.D. Jakes / by Sam Wellman.
   p. cm. — (Black Americans of achievement)
Includes bibliographical references and index.
Summary: A biography of the dynamic African-American religious
leader and author of best-selling inspirational books.
ISBN 0-7910-5362-8
      0-7910-5363-6 (pbk.)
1. Jakes, T. D. Juvenile literature. 2. Afro-American clergy Biography
Juvenile literature. 3. Afro-American Baptists Biography Juvenile liter-
ature. 4. Baptists—United States—Clergy Biography Juvenile litera-
ture. [1. Jakes, T. D. 2. Clergy. 3. Afro-Americans Biography.] I. Title.
II. Series.
BX6455.J25W45 1999
289.9'4'092—dc21   99-30676
[B]   CIP

CONTENTS

BLACK AMERICANS OF ACHIEVEMENT

HENRY AARON
baseball great

KAREEM ABDUL-JABBAR
basketball great

MUHAMMAD ALI
heavyweight champion

RICHARD ALLEN
religious leader and social activist

MAYA ANGELOU
author

LOUIS ARMSTRONG
musician

ARTHUR ASHE
tennis great

JOSEPHINE BAKER
entertainer

JAMES BALDWIN
author

TYRA BANKS
model

BENJAMIN BANNEKER
scientist and mathematician

COUNT BASIE
bandleader and composer

ANGELA BASSETT
actress

ROMARE BEARDEN
artist

HALLE BERRY
actress

MARY MCLEOD BETHUNE
educator

GEORGE WASHINGTON
CARVER
botanist

JOHNNIE COCHRAN
lawyer

SEAN "PUFFY" COMBS
music producer

BILL COSBY
entertainer

MILES DAVIS
musician

FREDERICK DOUGLASS
abolitionist editor

CHARLES DREW
physician

W. E. B. DU BOIS
scholar and activist

PAUL LAURENCE DUNBAR
poet

DUKE ELLINGTON
bandleader and composer

RALPH ELLISON
author

JULIUS ERVING
basketball great

LOUIS FARRAKHAN
political activist

ELLA FITZGERALD
singer

ARETHA FRANKLIN
entertainer

MORGAN FREEMAN
actor

MARCUS GARVEY
black nationalist leader

JOSH GIBSON
baseball great

WHOOPI GOLDBERG
entertainer

CUBA GOODING JR.
actor

ALEX HALEY
author

PRINCE HALL
social reformer

JIMI HENDRIX
musician

MATTHEW HENSON
explorer

GREGORY HINES
performer

BILLIE HOLIDAY
singer

LENA HORNE
entertainer

WHITNEY HOUSTON
singer and actress

LANGSTON HUGHES
poet

JANET JACKSON
musician

JESSE JACKSON
civil-rights leader and politician

MICHAEL JACKSON
entertainer

SAMUEL L. JACKSON *actor*	JOE LOUIS *heavyweight champion*	ROSA PARKS *civil-rights leader*	TINA TURNER *entertainer*
T. D. JAKES *religious leader*	RONALD MCNAIR *astronaut*	COLIN POWELL *military leader*	ALICE WALKER *author*
JACK JOHNSON *heavyweight champion*	MALCOLM X *militant black leader*	PAUL ROBESON *singer and actor*	MADAM C. J. WALKER *entrepreneur*
MAGIC JOHNSON *basketball great*	BOB MARLEY *musician*	JACKIE ROBINSON *baseball great*	BOOKER T. WASHINGTON *educator*
SCOTT JOPLIN *composer*	THURGOOD MARSHALL *Supreme Court justice*	CHRIS ROCK *comedian and actor*	DENZEL WASHINGTON *actor*
BARBARA JORDAN *politician*	TERRY MCMILLAN *author*	DIANA ROSS *entertainer*	J. C. WATTS *politician*
MICHAEL JORDAN *basketball great*	TONI MORRISON *author*	WILL SMITH *actor*	VANESSA WILLIAMS *singer and actress*
CORETTA SCOTT KING *civil-rights leader*	ELIJAH MUHAMMAD *religious leader*	WESLEY SNIPES *actor*	OPRAH WINFREY *entertainer*
MARTIN LUTHER KING, JR. *civil-rights leader*	EDDIE MURPHY *entertainer*	CLARENCE THOMAS *Supreme Court justice*	TIGER WOODS *golf star*
LEWIS LATIMER *scientist*	JESSE OWENS *champion athlete*	SOJOURNER TRUTH *antislavery activist*	RICHARD WRIGHT *author*
SPIKE LEE *filmmaker*	SATCHEL PAIGE *baseball great*	HARRIET TUBMAN *antislavery activist*	
CARL LEWIS *champion athlete*	CHARLIE PARKER *musician*	NAT TURNER *slave revolt leader*	

ON
ACHIEVEMENT

———— ❦ ————

Coretta Scott King

Before you begin this book, I hope you will ask yourself what the word *excellence* means to you. I think it's a question we should all ask, and keep asking as we grow older and change. Because the truest answer to it should never change. When you think of excellence, perhaps you think of success at work; or of becoming wealthy; or meeting the right person, getting married, and having a good family life.

Those goals are worth striving for, but there is a better way to look at excellence. As Martin Luther King Jr. said in one of his last sermons, "I want you to be first in love. I want you to be first in moral excellence. I want you to be first in generosity. If you want to be important, wonderful. If you want to be great, wonderful. But recognize that he who is greatest among you shall be your servant."

My husband knew that the true meaning of achievement is service. When I met him, in 1952, he was already ordained as a Baptist minister and was working toward a doctoral degree at Boston University. I was studying at the New England Conservatory and dreamed of accomplishments in music. We married a year later, and after I graduated the following year we moved to Montgomery, Alabama. We didn't know it then, but our notions of achievement were about to undergo a dramatic change.

You may have read or heard about what happened next. What began with the boycott of a local bus line grew into a national crusade, and by the time he was assassinated in 1968 my husband had fashioned a black movement powerful enough to shatter forever the practice of racial segregation. What you may not have read about is where he learned to resist injustice without compromising his religious beliefs.

He adopted a strategy of nonviolence from a man of a different race, who lived in a different country and even practiced a different religion. The man was Mahatma Gandhi, the great leader of India, who devoted his life to serving humanity in the spirit of love and nonviolence. It was in these principles that Martin discovered his method for social reform. More than anything else, those two principles were the key to his achievements.

These books are about African Americans who served society through the excellence of their achievements. They form part of the rich history of black men and women in America—a history of stunning accomplishments in every field of human endeavor, from literature and art to science, industry, education, diplomacy, athletics, jurisprudence, even polar exploration.

Not all of the people in this history had the same ideals, but I think you will find that all of them had something in common. Like Martin Luther King Jr., they all decided to become "drum majors" and serve humanity. In that principle—whether it was expressed in books, inventions, or song—they found a goal and a guide outside themselves that showed them a way to serve others instead of living only for themselves.

Reading the stories of these courageous men and women not only helps us discover the principles that we will use to guide our own lives; it also teaches us about our black heritage and about America itself. It is crucial for us to know the heroes and heroines of our history and to realize that the price we paid in our struggle for equality in America was dear. But we must also understand that we have gotten as far as we have partly because America's democratic system and ideals made it possible.

We are still struggling with racism and prejudice. But the great men and women in this series are a tribute to the spirit of the country in which they have flourished. And that makes their stories special and worth knowing.

1

GLORIOUS TURNAROUND

Bishop T. D. Jakes (right) baptizes superstar athlete Deion Sanders on October 19, 1997. The conversion to Christianity of the high-profile Dallas Cowboys' star drew national attention to Jakes and his Dallas-based church, The Potter's House.

OCTOBER 19, 1997, was an eventful Sunday in Dallas, Texas. The city's professional football team— the Dallas Cowboys—had defeated the Jacksonville Jaguars at Texas Stadium. Would that victory mark a turnaround for the football team that had stumbled along for two years since winning Super Bowl XXX? Before the Jacksonville game the Cowboys had lost as many games during the 1997 season as they had won.

It was too soon to tell if the victory over Jacksonville meant the Cowboys' season was turning around, but Deion Sanders and three other members of the team definitely felt they had experienced a turnaround. Their feelings had little to do with football. That Sunday evening the four stood inside The Potter's House, an enormous barnlike church 10 miles south of Texas Stadium.

"We're excited about what God is doing in the lives of these men," boomed a huge man in a collarless white robe. "They just won this game, and most of the time after winning a game they'd be out partying—but look at what the Lord has done!"

The pastor, his calling revealed by black crosses on his long sleeves, was taller than most of the football players standing near him. The six-foot, three-inch pastor was Thomas Dexter Jakes, known as Bishop Jakes or Pastor Jakes or often simply as T. D. Jakes. The pastor and the four players were all

African American, but the congregation was diverse: black, Hispanic, and white. Many members of the congregation were there to see T. D. Jakes baptize the players that night.

Baptism is an ancient custom in which water is used to symbolically wash away sins. In Christian churches, it is a way to publicly profess faith in Jesus Christ, often as part of being accepted into the church. So when T. D. Jakes baptized the players, they were making a religious commitment to Christ.

In T. D. Jakes's church the new members were actually immersed in a tank of water. One by one the players entered the tank. Each man pinched his nose; then the huge pastor plunged him under the water, then yanked him up again. After all four were baptized, the thoroughly soaked players huddled together outside the tank, weeping with joy. In their minds they had experienced the greatest turnaround possible.

Afterward, Emmitt Smith, one of the best running backs in professional football, shot both hands into the sky just as if he had scored a touchdown. Today's young people, he said later, need the Bible's answers more than they need anything they can learn from an athlete, a teacher, or a parent. The Bible, Smith affirmed, is the Word of God, and the final authority for all Christian conduct. Emmitt's firm belief in the Bible was based on the teachings of his spiritual mentor, T. D. Jakes.

Defensive back Omar Stoutmire had sealed the Cowboy victory that day by intercepting a pass with only a minute left in the game. It was the best game the 23-year-old rookie from California had ever played. But after his baptism Omar knew whom to thank for his blessings. "Anyone who doesn't know the Lord may seem like they are okay, but they are really living in darkness" Stoutmire said in a press release. "I thank the Lord for allowing me to play football, so that I may uplift His name." Teammate George Hegiman agreed. "I want the world to know

what God has done for me as a person under His will," he said.

The fourth Dallas Cowboy to be baptized was one of the biggest stars in sports, Deion Sanders. Of all the converts, Deion was the most unexpected. Deion was a lightning rod for both admiration and resentment, a man few people would ever regard as humble. He had made a career out of bragging about himself. He was the flaunting, taunting "hot dog," who bragged he could do something, then did it, and then bragged some more.

Now this megastar was humbly speaking about

Emmitt Smith, the Dallas Cowboys' star running back, scores a touchdown over the Jacksonville Jaguars' defensive line on October 19, 1997. Smith was one of four Cowboys baptized at The Potter's House after the team's victory that night.

his new faith. "I have not cleansed myself of all the wrongdoings and evil things," Sanders admitted. "[But] I've buried the old Deion Sanders; there is a new one walking strong and healthy because of what the Lord has done in my life. Football is a game—but this is eternal."

For many years, Deion had treated life as a game. He was the premiere defensive back in professional football. Any pass thrown by the opposition into his defensive territory was as likely to be intercepted by him as it was to be completed to the opposing receiver. In his first nine years he intercepted 36 passes, running 8 back for touchdowns. But Deion didn't stop there. He ran back punts and kickoffs as well as he played defense. He had eight touchdowns to his credit by running back kicks. He didn't stop there either. On occasion he played wide receiver on offense too; he was so versatile and so successful at playing football that he antagonized opposing teams and their fans into a frenzy.

And his accomplishments didn't stop even there. Not only did he dazzle on the football field but he scintillated on the baseball diamond too. Astonishingly, he played two professional sports and not just adequately; he excelled. In professional baseball he was a speed demon, specializing in triples and stolen bases.

As a result, Deion was infuriating to the opposition. To make matters worse for his opponents in both football and baseball, he glorified himself with nicknames like "Neon Deion" and "Prime Time." He spelled his last name with a dollar sign: $anders. He flaunted heavy gold chains and flashy, expensive clothes; he made an album called *Prime Time* that made the R&B charts; and he even toured with the vocal group Boyz II Men for a time. Yes, there was a lot of success there for people to envy and fume about.

Was Deion at long last humbled? Had he truly buried the old strutting Deion? When he first announced in June 1997 that he had found religion, there were many skeptics who said this was just another way for obnoxious Deion to get attention. Sanders denied these allegations, telling the *Dallas Morning News*, "The naysayers, the doubters, the nonbelievers, the persecutors, those people—they've just got to realize I know who I am and I know what I was. And that's a heck of a difference."

Still, Deion knew he had to *show* his life was different. So he visited churches. He talked to youth groups. He emphasized that in spite of his glitzy reputation, he had never smoked a cigarette, never so much as sipped alcohol, never used illegal drugs. Yet he had succumbed to another addiction: fame and fortune. He had reveled in it. And with fame came temptation. By being unfaithful to his wife he had lost her and his two children. Public success had so ruined his private life that he had actually thought of the ultimate act of desperation: suicide. Deion gave his newfound faith the credit for his rescue from suicidal depression.

In the first months before his baptism, Deion was well received in local Dallas churches. T. D. Jakes, Deion's mentor, cautioned the church members not to pay too much attention to Deion. He was just a "baby Christian," Jakes reminded, who needed to be taught more about the Bible. If Christians were too excited about Deion, they might keep him from growing in his new faith.

But just as T. D. Jakes cautioned those who gave Deion too much credit, he blasted those who gave the star athlete too little credit. One month before the baptism, T. D. Jakes had to reprimand cynical critics of Deion. In the *Dallas Morning News*, he wrote:

> Dallas Cowboy Deion Sanders' joyful proclamation of his religious conversion has been met with a torrent of disdain and incredulity among reporters.
>
> Though I am a Christian, I realize there always will be those who don't agree with Mr. Sanders' reli-

T. D. Jakes's style of delivering his sermons, in which he walks the pulpit, scolding, imploring, and exhorting his listeners, has made him one of the most popular Pentecostal preachers today.

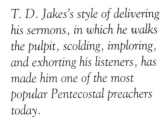

gious views. That is part of our rights as Americans.

However, there is cause for concern when we become cynical about someone even attempting to aspire to something that is, at the very least, a moral improvement. . . . let's pray that we never see the day that we become so cynical that we receive good news with the same disdain that we receive the bad. The public should rally behind and support [Deion].

Pastor T. D. Jakes was a tower of strength for Deion. Later Deion unashamedly confessed that although he had both a biological father and a step-father, Jakes was the first man he'd ever called "Daddy."

In his testimony that Sunday evening, after being baptized, Deion repeated the words of Jesus in the Bible: "For what shall it profit a man, if he shall gain the whole world, and lose his own soul?"

In the minds of many, Deion wasn't the only one who needed his soul saved. Other Dallas Cowboy players seemed in constant trouble. Allegations of drug use, abusing women, and other crimes were always surfacing about the Cowboys. Even the team's head coach had gotten into trouble, when he was caught carrying a concealed weapon aboard a plane. For those reasons, many people who heard the news of the four baptisms welcomed this sign of some Cowboys looking for spiritual answers and "redemption."

What was this church that redeemed these young men?

Jakes's church was called The Potter's House. The name comes from the Bible's Book of Jeremiah, in which God says to the prophet, "Arise, and go down to the potter's house, and there I will cause thee to hear my words." And there in the potter's house Jeremiah sees a potter reshape an ugly, useless vessel into a beautiful, useful one. Then God says, "Cannot I do with you as this potter [did with this vessel]? Indeed, like clay in the hands of the potter, so are you in my hand."

So The Potter's House was a church where God reshaped useless humans into useful ones. And who was its pastor, T. D. Jakes? Yes, who was this huge pastor who could dunk, then haul these football players—even 330-pound George Hegiman—out of the baptismal tank like rag dolls?

2

WEST VIRGINIA ROOTS

❧

THOMAS DEXTER JAKES was born June 9, 1957, in Vandalia, a tiny village in West Virginia just outside Charleston. His parents, Ernest and Odith Jakes, already had a son and a daughter. Thomas's earliest memories of his parents were warm. His father fascinated him, particularly because he was so hairy. Thomas used to check his own bald chest every now and then to see if any peach fuzz had grown yet. His father was his role model, the image of whom he one day hoped to be.

Many years later, in his book *Naked and Not Ashamed*, Thomas recalls "what it was like to fall asleep watching television and have my father pick up my listless, sleep-ridden frame from the couch and carry me up the stairs to bed. I would wake up to the faint smell of his 'Old Spice' cologne and feel his strong arms around me, carrying me as if I weighed nothing at all. I never felt as safe and protected as I did in the arms of my father."

Thomas's mother also made his childhood memories golden. "Every Sunday morning," he reminisces in *Can You Stand to Be Blessed?*, "my mother would go into the kitchen while we were still asleep and begin making homemade waffles for breakfast. These were real waffles. I don't remember all the ingredients she had in them, but I do remember that this particular recipe required beating the egg whites and

Thomas Dexter Jakes grew up in a small rural town near Charleston, West Virginia. He was the third child of Ernest and Odith Jakes.

then folding them into the waffle batter. . . . When I would rise, clad in a pair of worn pajamas and scuffy shoes, the smell of waffles would fill the room with the kind of aroma that made you float out of the bed. I can still see that old waffle iron. It was round and had an old cord that was thick and striped. . . . The waffle would begin to steam and hiss [and] . . . push that lid up as if the waffle had been sleeping too and decided to rise. There was no doubt in anybody's mind that they were done. They smelled like Hallelujah and they looked like glory to God. . . . Breakfast on Sunday morning was a religious experience."

Thomas regarded his mother with wonder—and with good reason. Odith Jakes had graduated from high school at age 15 and entered Tuskegee University, where she earned a bachelor's degree, studying home economics. This was quite an accomplishment for an African-American woman in the 1940s, but Odith did not stop there. She continued her education at the West Virginia School of Graduate Studies, earning a master's degree in psychology. She taught home economics in school for several years in Muncie, Indiana; Hattiesburg, Mississippi; and Charleston, while also taking care of the house and raising Thomas and his two siblings.

In *Daddy Loves His Girls*, T. D. Jakes writes, "[Mother] could bake a birthday cake while talking on the phone—without a mixer. I can still see her robust arms trembling as she creamed the four rigid sticks of butter into the mountain of sugar that she had placed in the bowl and beat with a spoon turned flat down in the bowl. Not only that, she could heat food without a microwave. I remember her cooking many roasts on top of a broken stove that should have been thrown away. Without much help she could take twenty-five dollars and a bus ticket and go to the grocery store with three children clutching her cotton dress. She would come back with a week's worth of groceries and cook the dinner before five without packaged food or processed meats. I am so thankful I have seen real parenting."

T. D. Jakes later described his mother as "the stream from which I emanated, the root from which I was derived, and the compass that influenced my course." His father Ernest also influenced young Thomas; both parents instilled in him a strong work ethic at an early age. Ernest Jakes started his own janitorial business with just a mop and bucket, and through long hours of hard work built the company into a 42-employee operation that cleaned everything from Charleston grocery stores to the West Virginia state government offices. Odith helped her husband run the business.

Thomas was only dimly aware at first that his father worked almost every waking hour. Yet it was no accident that one of his most frequent memories was his father carrying him to bed. His father probably had just come home from working all day and late into the evening. "He worked so much that the children and I seldom saw him," said Odith Jakes. "Those were hard times. He worked several jobs."

Thomas's mother was the one who was always there for the three children. And she had rules for herself that were helpful. "I learned that listening was far better than talking. You need to be able to track and understand your children," Odith later admitted. "I practiced never taking my frustrations out on them. I taught them to shoot for the top. I taught them to be all they could be. I remember telling them, 'If you become a street sweeper, be the best one on the road. If you become a teacher, be the best one in the school.' I guess I was a motivator to them. I tried to be one. I always taught them they could do anything if they tried hard enough."

Thomas has verified that her "rules" were very effective. His mother always listened closely to him when he talked. Her attention "dignified" his opinion. Her actions confirmed to him that he mattered.

As a young boy, Thomas enjoyed playing games on the rolling hills around his town, taking music lessons, and watching the broad Kanawha River (pictured here) flow toward Charleston.

Her careful, patient listening gave him self-esteem. Regardless of whether she agreed or didn't agree with what he said, he was always excited that she listened to him.

Because his mother was a teacher and doted on her own children, it was no surprise that young Thomas was already reading and writing before he started school. And because she taught home economics, it was no surprise either that Thomas could clean house, sew, and cook. He never thought of these skills as chores that only his mother and sister Jackie did. His older brother, Ernest Jr., had to do them too.

In his early years Thomas often accompanied his mother to women's clubs, where Odith Jakes was a guest speaker. After one of these occasions six-year-old Thomas revealed a fire that already burned inside him. "The time will come when you will travel with me and I will speak!" he told his mother.

Thomas's mother and father had come to West Virginia from the Deep South, a distant place they fondly recollected when the bitter winter winds blew snow outside their house. Painful memories were evoked, however, whenever anyone spoke about African-American experiences with voting, making a living, or law enforcement. To Thomas, the Deep South sounded like a land in a fairy tale that was tropical but wicked. Could such a place exist? Yes, apparently it did. African Americans in Vandalia often spoke of it, but Thomas was far too busy as a child to reflect much on what they were saying.

Bit by bit, young Thomas learned about his roots. Odith was the youngest of seven girls among 15 siblings. She had been raised in Marion, Alabama, where she attended high school with a girl named Coretta Scott, later the wife of civil rights leader Martin Luther King. Ernest Jakes, one of three children, was from Waynesboro, Mississippi, just about 100 miles away from Marion. He had met Odith in Hattiesburg, Mississippi, after she had finished college and was working as a teacher. Ernest had two years of college himself, but he quit school to marry and support Odith. Like many African Americans in the Deep South during the 1950s, the young married couple migrated north, eventually settling in Vandalia, West Virginia.

The state seemed a welcoming place for African Americans. When the Civil War began in 1861, the western mountaineers in Virginia were unwilling to secede from the Union and join the slave states of the Confederacy. So they tore away from the Confederate state of Virginia to become the Union state of West Virginia—and they fought against slavery. The new state was heavily forested, and the timber and coal mining industries brought settlers to West Virginia. Decades after the state was established in 1863, the typical West Virginian was white, Christian, and a rural resident. Charleston itself was historic but not large for a state capital, with a population of about 60,000.

The area around Charleston yielded coal, gas, and oil. Local plants manufactured glass, chemicals, and metal products. Yet, although there were laboring jobs available, and Ernest had two years of college and manual skills, he had to scramble to get any kind of work. African American men had a hard time finding decent jobs, even in West Virginia.

But as a child, Thomas did not realize that his family was struggling. Although the Jakes family lived in a simple two-bedroom house, Thomas did not even know he was poor. He admitted years later that his poverty "was not the kind of poverty that required sympathy. Our poverty was veiled by the fact that we were living like most of our neighbors. We were therefore oblivious to the fact that other Americans were eating real eggs rather than powdered ones. I never noticed that I wore little home-made shirts while the other children from more affluent neighborhoods wore brand-name clothes to school. It never crossed my mind that spaghetti should have meatballs. In short, we were together, and consequently we were happy."

Thomas enjoyed life as a schoolboy. Vandalia was a hillside community of African Americans, and the families that lived there were united by a desire to survive. Young Thomas was protected not only by his father, mother, older brother Ernest Jr., and older sister Jackie, but also by the neighbors. However, he did not always appreciate their attention. Some of his neighbors seemed nosy to the young boy, particularly when they called his parents if he got into any mischief. At times he resented the neighbors—but he also respected them.

Thomas had hardworking, church-going parents, but he was no angel. He wrestled with right and

At an early age, and with the urging of his parents, T. D. Jakes began reading the Bible and memorizing scripture passages.

wrong. In his early school years he and his friends made some bad decisions. One trick was to go into a store and purchase certain merchandise after he had switched the price tag with the tag from a lower-cost item. Because Thomas paid for his "discounted" item, he deluded himself into thinking he was not stealing. Later, he decided what he was doing was wrong, and he stopped.

But he certainly enjoyed those early school years and his friends. "The best parts of school when I was an eight-year-old were recess and the walk home from school," he recalls fondly in *Naked and Not Ashamed*:

> I liked recess because it gave me an opportunity to stretch my legs and play with my friends. I liked the walk home from school because I usually had a quarter buried deep within my pocket, hidden somewhere

beneath the bubble gum, the baseball cards, and all the other paraphernalia that eight-year-olds think are valuable. I would save that quarter until we walked down Troy Road toward [the store of] 'old man Harless.' . . . Now, that was what we called him if we were sure he wasn't around. But if we saw him, he immediately became 'Mr. Harless,' complete with 'Yes, sir,' and 'No, sir,' and all the other polite things we were instructed to say lest the seats of our pants perish in the fires of my mother's wrath! That quarter of mine was saved for the brightly colored books that were stacked in a display for all the children to see. There were all of my old friends—Superman and Captain Marvel, Captain America and Spiderman. I would purchase a copy of the latest issue and hurry a little farther down Troy Road. Once I found the old path that led up the hill behind the house, I would start my ascent to the big rock beneath the apple tree. There, hidden from public scrutiny, I would pull out my prized hero magazine and imagine that I was one of these men, a super hero who could transform as needed into anything necessary to destroy the villain. . . . I grew up reading about heroes. We believed in possibility, and though we were neither wealthy nor affluent, we could escape like a bird through the window of a full-color magazine and become anybody we wanted to be for at least 30 minutes—before my mother's voice would be heard from the rickety back porch behind the house.

Life was joyful year-round for Thomas. When winter sledding was over, he happily put his sled away and planned a thousand things for spring. He had boundless energy. He ran up and down the rugged green hills in the summer. He sat and looked down on the wide Kanawha River. Folks said boats could navigate it all the way northwest to Point Pleasant on the mighty Ohio River where Daniel Boone had once lived. To the north, across the Kanawha River, he could see the brick buildings of downtown Charleston, where his father often went to work.

Thomas often played with his friends after school. Their games were simple ones that required teamwork and lots of interaction. The teams shared victories and defeats; they strategized how to defeat the other team. The boys told each other secrets, and they huddled together to plan how to overcome the other team's defenses. They were fascinated with frogs, and they thought girls were silly when they shrieked and ran away from a toad or some other animal.

When Thomas and his friends played in the yard behind the Jakes' house, they kept cautious eyes on the family dog that Thomas's father called "Pup." Pup was mean and ferocious and would bite anyone who came near him. He was chained in the back of the house to a four-by-four post, and the boys liked to stand just beyond the dog's reach and tease him. No, Thomas was no angel.

Eventually Thomas had to stop playing and go inside to practice his piano lessons. Then—with his roughneck friends gone—he could indulge himself in being his mother's youngest child. How he relished his mother discovering some small injury like a cut finger and carefully cleaning the wound.

Through no particular effort of his own, Thomas began to express a very definite personality. His church had taught him a sense of right and wrong. His mother had instilled in him a belief he could accomplish anything. His father had taught him that he must be busy, busy, busy. So young Thomas was righteous, assertive, and active. A Vandalia neighbor, Bobby Tolliver, attested years later that "you could hear it all over the street" when young Thomas was in his house practicing Scripture memorization with his foghorn voice. And he was "kind of pushy."

But what did he push? Well, he sold newspapers and home-grown vegetables. At the age of nine Thomas grew greens in the family garden—which was well-protected by Pup. He sold the greens for $1 a bag, and even issued a receipt. Nosy neighbors and passersby were assaulted by his sales pitch. Few could refuse his insistence.

But these golden days would soon come to an end.

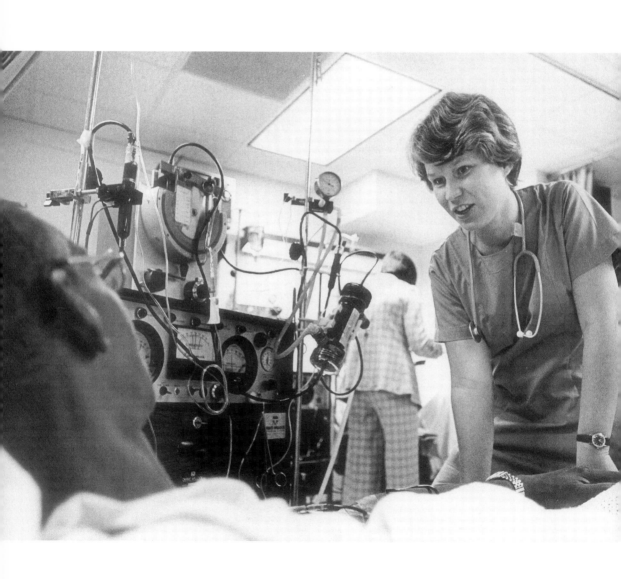

3

HEARTBREAK

THOMAS'S FATHER, Ernest Jakes, was an enormous man, weighing nearly 300 pounds. Thomas was about 10 when his dad went to the doctor for a physical examination because he was not feeling well. The doctor measured Mr. Jakes's blood pressure. To do this, two readings are taken, one while the heart is contracted and one while it is relaxed. A normal blood-pressure reading is around 120/80; Ernest's readings were 190/150, so his blood pressure was dangerously high. (For some unknown reason African American men are very susceptible to high blood pressure when they get older.)

High blood pressure has no symptoms in its early stages; that is why it is called the "silent killer." The only early symptom of Ernest's high blood pressure was bloating in his legs. This condition, caused by water retention, is called edema. Further tests after his physical examination revealed that the many years of uncontrolled high blood pressure had damaged Ernest's kidneys. Treatment had to begin at once.

Normally, kidneys filter waste products from the blood and release them into the urine, which is then removed from the body. Because Ernest's kidneys were damaged, they could not remove the toxins from his blood. The waste products had built up in his body until he was poisoning himself.

A person with high blood pressure can do a few

A nurse speaks with a diabetic patient who is hooked to a kidney dialysis machine. Diabetes slowly drained Ernest Jakes's strength, eventually killing the large, warm-hearted man. Thomas was deeply wounded by the loss of his father; it was many years before he could come to grips with his feelings about the traumatic incident.

things to help himself. He can eat a low-protein diet and drink lots of cranberry juice. (Cranberry juice is a natural diuretic that helps the kidneys remove the blood's waste products.) So Ernest guzzled cranberry juice by the gallon. But it was not enough. He needed dialysis too. Dialysis, a process that filters waste from the blood, is performed by a machine. The process has to be done two or three times a week in the hospital. If none of these procedures could stop the progressive damage to the kidneys, Ernest would pass into "end-stage kidney failure." Thomas was numbed by this news; he didn't want to believe the dread prognosis.

In the late 1960s when Ernest's doctors pronounced he was in end-stage kidney failure, there was no hope of a kidney transplant. This type of organ replacement did not yet exist. The final defense against the disease was use of a dialysis machine in the home. There the patient became almost permanently attached to the equipment. To operate the dialysis machine and take care of the patient, plenty of help was needed. In a family that could not afford professional nursing, everyone had to help. This work was not only exhausting and hard to stomach; it was heartbreaking. Ernest Jakes Sr. was doomed. Thomas's father was dying.

Before his family's eyes, the large, hardworking man began to physically break down. He lost weight. Day by day he grew weaker. All the while he suffered the many symptoms of the disease's last stages: headaches, chronic fatigue, nausea, diarrhea, itchy skin. Ernest's suffering took all these forms and was unrelieved. Thomas saw all this suffering, because he helped take care of his father too.

"I grew up suspended somewhere between life and death," recalled Thomas years later. Through this difficult experience he learned compassion.

He bathed his father. He shaved him. He mopped up blood that spilled from the dialysis apparatus. He stayed with his father at night. Thomas would awake terrified whenever the machine screeched its alarm that it required attention. He would jump up, groggy-headed, to attend to it.

As his father dwindled away, month after month, year after year, Thomas's exuberance and assertiveness ebbed and flowed. This terrible injustice was not supposed to happen. He could accept his role as caretaker for his father, but he could not accept the unfairness that made it necessary. Nor did he in any way assume that he was being tempered by this trial of fire. It was not about him; it was about his father dying.

When he was not helping care for his father, he would help make money for the family. Thomas would at times take to the streets full of optimism to sell Avon products. And he was persistent. "He could convince the devil himself to buy," asserted Vandalia neighbor Bobby Tolliver in a *Wall Street Journal* article.

But these bursts of activity on Thomas's part did not prevent the inevitable death of his father. When Thomas was 16, after six years of suffering, Ernest stopped breathing. He was dead. The giant, the strong behemoth who Thomas had thought was Hercules, was withered and dead at only 48 years of age!

In cases of terminal illnesses, coupled with the loss of the loved one is always the unspoken, hidden relief that the long, exhausting ordeal is finally over. Thomas tried to repress that terrible, selfish feeling— but the feeling of relief remained, even though deeply buried. So Thomas felt guilty. More guilt came as he wondered why he should survive when his father had died. Why did Thomas deserve to live? Why did his father have to die?

After the death of Ernest Jakes, Thomas sought answers in the Baptist church. The Baptists are the largest Protestant denomination in the United States; traditionally, many African Americans, such as the woman meditating here, have been members of Baptist churches.

These heavy concerns weighed down 16-year-old Thomas. He sought answers in his church. Thomas had been raised in the Baptist church, a Christian denomination with a very large membership. In its various branches the Baptist denomination embraced well over 20 million members in 1973. It had a history that went back 400 years to the Reformation, the revolution that split "Protestants"—those who protested against some established Christian practices—from the Catholic church. The earliest creed of the Protestants was simple and three-pronged. First, they believed authority was from the Holy Bible, not from church officials. Second, they believed a Christian was saved by faith in Jesus Christ, not by good works. Third, they believed church officials should come from the congregation, not from a formal hierarchy of priests.

In the earliest days Baptists distinguished themselves from other Protestants by believing that membership in their church was voluntary and that baptism of infants was not a biblical teaching. Only a person old enough to knowingly make decisions could profess faith in Jesus Christ. The Baptists have only two official religious rites. Baptism by immersion under water is a profession of faith in Christ and entitles the adult new believer to membership in the church. The second rite, which is shared by most Christian denominations, is the "Lord's Supper," the rite some Christians call the Eucharist or Holy Communion, in which Baptist church officials administer wine and bread to the faithful. This rite is directly from the teachings of Jesus himself, revealed at the "Last Supper," which is described in the Book of Luke:

> And he took bread, and gave thanks, and brake it, and gave unto them (his disciples), saying, This is my body which is given for you: this do in remembrance of me. Likewise also the cup after supper, saying, This cup is the new testament in my blood, which is shed for you. (Luke 22:19-20, King James Version)

Baptists try to avoid building up an organized church hierarchy of officials. As a result, each of the local churches is independent of other Baptist churches. This independence has always appealed to African Americans. At least, they have argued, their church is their own, even if nothing else is. So Thomas wasn't surprised to learn that in 1973 nearly 10 million African Americans were Baptists.

But he was not so naive that he did not see controversial issues among Baptists. Although they had been progressive enough to establish top colleges like Wake Forest, Brown, Temple, Colgate, and Baylor, they still had no women pastors. Thomas had to wonder about that. Why weren't women able to pastor? Where did the Bible—the ultimate authority of conduct—say that women could not pastor?

Thomas had certainly grown into very complex person with a thousand thoughts. He also admitted to himself that he had resented his father. Thomas faced the fact that his father had neglected him before he became so sick.

It would be a long time before Thomas could rationalize his feelings. Years later he wrote them all down in *Help! I'm Raising My Children Alone*:

I realize in retrospect that my father, who was a marvelous man, was busy trying to maneuver our family into economic stability. That was no easy feat for a black man in the fifties and sixties. He worked around the clock for peanuts. I understand why now. At the time, I just missed his affirmation. I thought he didn't want to be bothered. He had allowed my mother to assume areas that he should have maintained. He had become a ghost parent. He was there in spirit, but his flesh was long gone. He was absent from the football games and the concerts. Eventually I became accustomed to his faintly fading image disappearing through the door, always rushing out to fix something somewhere else—anywhere else but home. As the door slammed, the house shook, the floor vibrated and I . . . well, I just wondered what it would be like to go fishing or boating or anything that all the other children seemed to do with their dads. He was a ghost parent to me. . . . My dad is dead now. I respect him more in death than I understood him in life. I guess it is because now I have the responsibilities and the needs and the bills.

The emotional absence of Thomas's father during his son's early years would help him to counsel parents and families when he became an adult. He could understand the needs of one-parent families, for he had experienced what it was like to live with the attention of only his mother. She was the one who had been forced to do everything and be everything that the family needed. She was the one who attended band concerts and football games, who broke up fights and handled school problems.

All that his mother had done eventually helped to give Thomas a deep understanding and appreciation for women. He also came to recognize his own neglect of his mother. After being angry at his father so long for neglecting the family, an unsettling thought finally occurred to him one day: wasn't *he* guilty of neglect too? As much as Thomas adored his mother, he realized only later that he had scarcely ever acknowledged all her efforts. Yes, his father had neglected his needs. But how often had Thomas neglected his mother's needs? Probably a thousand times. How often had he thanked her? One time out of one hundred? And yet she had persevered.

This too he wrote about years later in *Help! I'm Raising My Children Alone*. God does not often send angels to the earth anymore, Thomas wrote, nor does he send prophets. Instead, God gives children parents who truly care about them, who take the time to listen and share, pray and give. These sorts of parents change the world, Thomas said; they do far more than the most eloquent preachers. In later years, Thomas would feel called to encourage and affirm these brave and loving parents who do so much.

Ernest Jakes's funeral was held in Waynesboro,

Mississippi. There, among the plowed fields of rusty red soil and the forests of soft green pines, Thomas met the matriarch of the Jakes family in Mississippi. His Grandmother Jakes had a robust frame and bountiful body, with strong arms and eyes that held "the burning embers of a fire, embers buried deep beneath the ashes of her experiences," remembers Thomas in his book *Naked and Not Ashamed.*

Yet, as the coffin bearing his father was being lowered into the grave, Thomas was overwhelmed by unmet needs. As he listened to the creak of the pulleys that eased his father's body into the red Mississippi clay, he realized that dead men can't talk and can't listen. He had a thousand unresolved issues still inside him as tears streamed down his face. He cried for the questions he would never get a chance to ask his father. He cried for all the times he would miss his father . . . and for his mother, who would never marry again. In spite of his father's flaws, he mourned his father deeply and sincerely. "How could he leave without saying good-bye?" he asked himself.

For 16-year-old T. D. Jakes, his father's death was devastating.

When his father had been healthy, Thomas had rarely seen him. Then when he finally had time with his father, the specter of death always cast its gloom. By the time his father died when Thomas was 16, the former ham-armed, 280-pound giant was only half his former weight. Seeing his great hulking father wasted away had wrenched Thomas's soul. But seeing him lowered into the earth was devastating.

4
INFILLING OF THE SPIRIT!

Many years after the death of his father, T. D. Jakes explained how he survived such a low point in his life: he rediscovered God, a whole God who loved to mend broken people.

Thomas began to crave Jesus. He admitted in a 1996 radio interview that although he had gone to church all his life—he had even served as its part-time music director—he was not a "good" person. He referred to himself as "a church sinner," someone who had been raised in a religious environment, yet lacked a personal experience with Jesus Christ. Now, however, Thomas began to long for something more. He was hungry for something that would give life more meaning. He began to look for God. He went to church with greater interest now, looking for real answers.

Eventually, Thomas developed a real relationship with God. As a result, Jesus became a part of Thomas's day-to-day existence. He depended on Christ to help him deal with life. He had just lost his father to kidney disease, and he felt abandoned and confused—but in Jesus, Thomas found the answers to his confusion.

Thomas was "born again" at a storefront Apostolic church. The Apostolic church is a branch of Christianity known as "Pentecostal." This denomination was born in America in the 20th century.

Bishop Jakes delivers an emotional speech to his congregation. As a young man, Thomas Dexter Jakes felt himself filled with the Holy Spirit when he joined the Pentecostal church during the painful period after his father's death.

Though many Pentecostal churches were small and poor when T. D. Jakes joined the church, this denomination of Christianity was growing faster than any other in America. Pentecostal churches were somewhat remarkable for their time: they embraced African Americans, Hispanics, and women not only as full members but also as ministers.

Amazingly, it seemed to have sprung up at the same time in several locations, mainly from Baptist and Methodist roots. Prominent African Americans like William Seymour, who headed the dynamic Azusa Street Revival in California, and Charles Harrison Mason, who led the Church of God in Christ in Mississippi, were a part of this movement. Pentecostals were remarkable for their time in that they embraced African Americans, Hispanics, and women not only as full members but even as ministers. Early African American women leaders included Elizabeth Mix, Magdalena Tate, and Ida Robinson.

Pentecostal beliefs differ from those of other denominations in that the believer experiences an "infilling of the Holy Spirit." Outsiders are often startled by the believer's frenzied outcries of what sounds like gibberish. But the believer is convinced it is the same experience as the miraculous "speaking of tongues" that the apostles experienced on the day of Pentecost, the time after Christ departed from this earth. All this is described in the book of the Bible called the Acts of the Apostles. Because the apostles' experience was on the day of Pentecost, the modern adherents of this infilling of the Holy Spirit have come to be known as "Pentecostals."

In the early 1970s, many Pentecostal churches were noted for being poor, down-and-out storefront enterprises. But the members had a fervor few other churches could instill. Thomas was not surprised to learn Pentecostals were thought to be the fastest-growing Christian denomination in America and probably in the world. The Pentecostals were even more fiercely independent than the Baptists, so it was hard to determine just how many members they had nationwide. Some said membership was in the millions.

Thomas learned that Pentecostalism was the Protestant denomination that had made the greatest impact on Catholic Latin America. Some said the explosion of Pentecostalism was the most significant religious event of the 20th century. Thomas knew the denomination appealed to African Americans because it offered independence, spiritual vigor, and adherence to the Bible. It was honest and progressive, and there were no barriers because of race or gender. Women were equals. In fact about 20 percent of the pastors were women. Some were even bishops.

Thomas was a thinker. He weighed all these things in his mind—but it was the infilling of the Holy Spirit that captured his soul. This experience gave rise to new cravings. For one thing, he became fascinated with the Bible. He told *Gospel Today* that he hungered for the Bible the way "a pregnant woman craves food." His desire for it was insatiable.

He smuggled the Bible into school, so he could read it all day long, hiding it inside his history and science textbooks. Kids began teasing him as the

"Bible Boy." They did no more than that because he was a mountainous youth, not one to rile. Rather than being hurt by the teasing, he felt proud—but he had to chastise himself for feeling too much pride.

Thomas began thinking about becoming a preacher. He walked around with his Bible in hand, alone or not, often preaching to the sky. But his pride soon evaporated under an onslaught of reality. At 17, Thomas saw himself as poor, gap-toothed, and homely with bad eyes. He even had a speech impediment. He had been so protected in his community he had scarcely been aware he spoke with a lisp—until now, when he needed speech the most. And he was so inexperienced. Surely he could never preach the Word. Thomas had lost the confidence he had had when he was a young boy and could sell anything to anyone. How would he ever be able to spread the gospel? Who would be attracted to him? Who would continue to listen after he lisped his first stumbling words?

During this time he finished high school and enrolled at nearby West Virginia State College in 1974. The urge to counsel, to help, was so strong that Thomas decided to fulfill that urge by studying to become a psychologist.

Of course he also had to work. Thomas drove a delivery truck one summer while he was in college. He had never driven a stick-shift vehicle before, and he ended up stalling the truck in the middle of traffic. Cars backed up behind him, horns honked, and Thomas panicked. Finally, he prayed for help and managed to get the car going. Afterward, he recalled that "my head was spinning, my pulse was weak and, to be blunt, my bladder was full!"

Preaching couldn't be any worse than that experience!

Still Thomas was reluctant to preach. He began to experience dreams and visions. In one vision, he felt God giving him a specific Bible verse that at the time he had not read: Jeremiah, chapter 1.

Two of the earliest Christian leaders were Peter and Paul. Peter had been one of Jesus' 12 apostles. According to the Acts of the Apostles in the Bible, after the death and resurrection of Jesus the apostles had been in a room together when tongues of fire appeared over their heads and all were filled with the Holy Spirit. This enabled them to go forth and preach Jesus' gospel. Paul had opposed Jesus until a personal experience opened his eyes; he eventually traveled throughout the known world spreading the gospel, and his letters provide a framework of rules for the church.

This Bible passage tells that when God called Jeremiah to preach, Jeremiah said he could not preach because he was a child. God responded: "Before I formed thee in the belly, I knew thee, and before thou camest forth out of the womb I sanctified thee, and I ordained thee prophet unto the nations." As a result of reading this biblical passage, Thomas eventually surrendered to what he believed to be God's call. Perhaps, like Jeremiah, Thomas Jakes would one day be a "prophet unto the nations."

Now Thomas was sure he must spread the gospel and help the hurting. But where would he start? What would he say? He dropped out of college, although he still had no pulpit. He was like a million itinerant preachers before him: when one does not have a pulpit, one preaches where the people are.

He was terrified. But preach he did, first on the

sidewalk, then once in a while in a makeshift church.

He said later in *Can You Stand to Be Blessed?*, "[A]round old coal stoves in tiny churches that never even considered buying a microphone . . . I learned how to preach. Often I would preach until sweaty and tired, to rows of empty pews with two or three people who decorated the otherwise empty church."

Did the luxury of a microphone help him? "Initially," he admitted in a *Gospel Today* interview, "I couldn't hold the microphone in my hand. I would have them adjust the stand for the microphone. I would put my hands behind my back, and lean forward and talk into the microphone because my hands shook so badly with fear."

He was not committed full-time to preaching the gospel. Thomas couldn't be—he still had to earn a living. He also continued to work on his college degree through correspondence courses. His father's blood must have been strong in him, for Thomas hardly thought anything about juggling several tasks at once. His persistence with preaching eventually paid off when he became a "part-time associate minister" at a local Pentecostal church. He was a "trouble-shooter," a "fill-in," a "sub," a "temp." With fear and trembling, he went to all the tiny Pentecostal churches.

He preached in places where other ministers would not go. He was willing to drive for hours to a rural, secluded "backwoods" area, where he would preach to a handful of poor people. Sometimes he was horrified by the conditions he encountered: flies and filth, broken beds, and slimy bathrooms. Sometimes, when he stayed overnight, he had to squeeze his six-foot, three-inch frame into the little bed of a ten-year-old girl who had given up her room for the traveling pastor, because the family had no extra bed. But through all these experiences, he felt God teaching him. Years later he wrote, "I thought I was traveling to minister to the people, but in actuality God was taking me through a series of hurdles and obstacles in order to strengthen my legs for the sprints ahead."

He had little more than his Bible, a beat-up old car, and the clothes on his back—but Thomas was well-read. And he knew he was in very good company: John Wesley, the founder of the Methodist church, had traveled far and wide to preach the gospel. And the earliest Christians, men like Peter and Paul, had spread the Word by traveling to distant cities to preach.

As T. D. Jakes continued preaching, he realized that he was getting better and better. The response of his listeners proved it. His knowledge of the Bible had been thorough from the beginning, and he had suffered much in his life, so he had no lack of examples for his sermons. All he had needed was a more effective delivery of his message, and this was improving every day. If he still had a lisp, no one seemed to notice. His intimidating appearance had become a plus. This was no preacher with whom to trifle. And by watching other Pentecostal preachers, Jakes developed his own unique style of preaching.

Bible in hand, he would stomp about the pulpit. He chanted. He scolded. He implored. He cried. He whooped. He exhorted. He crawled. He sang, interjecting rich Gospel music from the Baptist and Pentecostal traditions. He even sang portions of his sermon. His arms reached high in the universal Pentecostal symbol of surrender to Almighty God. His dynamic sermons made people respond emotionally and spiritually.

In 1980 Thomas became part-time pastor at the Temple of Faith, a Pentecostal church in Montgomery, West Virginia. Montgomery was a small town of 2,000 residents, half an hour southeast of Charleston. The church was an old storefront building cluttered with rickety chairs and torn-out theater seats. There was no pulpit. His congregation numbered 10 members.

Thomas and Serita Jamison Jakes at a 1999 conference in Atlanta. T. D. met his future wife while traveling through West Virginia and preaching.

But this handful of people turned out to be just the right number. The entire church could eat together at almost anyone's house. And that handful was about all that T. D. could handle when he was still only in his early twenties.

The young preacher went about his duties energetically. Thomas raised money for a pulpit. He laid a cinder-block baptismal tank. He managed to scrounge an old piano for services. Soon he was hammering the keys, singing hymns, and preaching from his new pulpit. He had been preaching now for several years, and his delivery was powerful. He glowed inside when his members brought newcomers into church. He knew from the looks on the newcomers' faces that they expected a real humdinger. He didn't disappoint them. "When T. D. Jakes opens his mouth, what comes out is liquid fire," said John Hagee, a fiery preacher himself. Thomas's preaching had a powerful impact on the lives of his listeners.

One of those whose life was changed by T. D. Jakes's preaching was his older brother, Ernest. A construction worker, Ernest had helped Thomas build the church's pulpit and baptismal font. At the same time, Thomas helped his older brother develop a relationship with God. "I would help [Thomas] with his dream, but I didn't belong to the Lord at that time—I didn't know that I belonged to the Lord," Ernest told the *Dallas Morning News* in January 1999. "I asked him one day, 'Is [Jesus] really real? Are you sure this is real?' And he said to me, 'This is more real than anything that I've ever seen in my life. I guarantee you this is real.'"

Thomas affected many others outside of his church as well. He continued to travel to small churches and rural areas to preach, because he and his small congregation needed the money. Thomas's financial situation was poor. Most of the time he was paid with food, cakes, and jars of jelly. If he was lucky, he got enough gas money to go home.

His suits were worn and shiny. And when they became dirty, he couldn't afford to have them dry-cleaned, so he had to launder them. Still, Thomas somehow impressed a young lady who lived in Beckley, West Virginia—30 miles from Montgomery, down the toll road, which of course he did not often have the money to use. Serita Ann Jamison began sending notes to him. The notes seemed to go beyond topics like righteousness and holiness. She was smitten with him.

Thomas had hardly expected anything like this. Who was this Serita? When he was introduced to

The Union Carbide plant in Charleston, West Virginia, where Thomas worked when he was not preaching, closed in 1982. This threw the family into deep financial trouble.

her, he couldn't believe his eyes. She was so pretty that his knees turned to jelly. He was frightened, and he resisted her interest. He explains in *Loose That Man and Let Him Go*, "Men struggle with commitment. When I met my wife, I knew in my heart that she was the one for me. Yet the hardest thing in the world for me was trying to get my lips to part and force my tongue to cooperate in forming the words, 'Let's get m-a . . . m-a-r . . . m-a-r-r-i-e-d!'"

When Thomas finally let Serita know he was interested in marrying her, she revealed she had real worries about marriage herself. She was just a coal miner's daughter. She was terrified of being a pastor's wife, a very demanding task. Serita couldn't have found a better way to commit Thomas if she had tried. Thomas was the counselor, the listener, the helper. Serita's doubt was something he could handle. He told her over and over, "You can do it."

By 1980 they were married. Soon after, Serita became pregnant. So the young couple found a small house in Vandalia, near Thomas's mother Odith. It was in Vandalia that Serita gave birth to twin boys. The young parents named their children Jamar and Jermaine.

To provide for his family, Thomas knew that he had to get a job that paid well. His new children couldn't live as itinerants. So he began working at the nearby Union Carbide chemical plant in Charleston. Thomas worked afternoons and nights. In his spare time, he still preached.

Sometimes he felt like he was his father all over again. He was working long hours at a difficult job to provide for his family. How many things could he do at one time? He did not want to neglect his wife and infant children.

Despite this, the Jakes family was happy until bad news came in 1982. Thomas found out Union Carbide was going to close its Charleston chemical plant. Uncertain times lay ahead.

5

RISING PASTOR

❦

AT AGE 25, THOMAS was like his father had been: absent from home, scraping, struggling, scratching to survive. Although his Temple of Faith congregation had grown from 10 to 40 members, after the Union Carbide plant closed he found himself slogging along the shoulders of roads, picking up bottles to sell.

His feelings of resentment toward his father began to soften. Now he too had a wife at home and tiny mouths to feed. The family was so poor it could not pay its bills. Soon the Jakeses had no gas, no water. Thomas had to trudge to his mother's house to fill containers with water, then lug them back to his own house.

Night after night, Thomas worried and prayed. His wife boiled water for baths, because the gas had been turned off. Sometimes the electricity was off too. He and his children wrapped up in quilts and huddled around a burning 55-gallon drum as the only source of heat. His car looked so bad that when guests came to his church, one of his deacons wanted to hide the car behind the building. At church, he sang and shouted, but inside he was shaking.

On one occasion Thomas's car broke down. He needed to get to the electricity company to ask them not to cut off the power again. He caught a bus to town, where he begged the company not to turn off

By 1983 Thomas's church had grown to more than 80 members. That year, residents of West Virginia who could not get to church to hear the popular preacher in person could listen to him speak about the gospel on a weekly radio program, The Master's Plan.

power to his home. The company cut it off anyway. He burst into tears. He was at the end of his rope.

But on the way home, Thomas heard the Lord. Thomas related later that God

> said in the rich tones of a clarinet-type voice, 'I will not suffer thy foot to be moved!' That was all He said, but it was how He said it that caused worship to flush the pain out of my heart. It was as if He were saying, 'Who do you think that I am? I will not suffer thy foot to be moved. Don't you understand that I love you?' I shall never forget as long as I live the holy hush and the peace of His promise that came into my spirit. Suddenly the light, the gas, and the money didn't matter. What mattered was I knew I was not alone.

The words Thomas heard were from Psalm 121, a passage that also promises, "The Lord shall preserve thy going out and thy coming in from this time forth, and even for evermore." Thomas believed that promise with all his heart and soul. So in spite of his worsening conditions, he still served his tiny church in Montgomery. He still preached the gospel in his worn-out suits. He still directed his tiny choir.

Now he often coordinated the hymns with his sermon. As the church members sang he interjected rhythmic quotes from the Bible. His bass voice rumbled like a volcano, and words of fire erupted.

Thomas was never idle. He would dig a ditch if he had the chance to earn some extra money. He still careened over the back roads of hilly West Virginia in his beat-up car (when it ran). He helped other pastors any way he could.

Serita fulfilled her role as the pastor's wife, acting as president of the usher board and also as worship leader. At the same time, she worked hard to take care of their twin sons. In later years she proudly labeled herself "an old-fashioned biblical-type wife."

"God speaks to my husband and gives directions to the family," she later told the *Dallas Morning News*.

"It's hard to articulate how much respect I have for my husband. I would never do anything to disrespect him. . . . I'm just hopelessly in love."

Thomas and Serita never saw themselves as insignificant and silly just because the congregation was small. As Bible students they knew holy obligations started small. Hadn't Jesus traveled the Holy Land with a mere 12 disciples? Besides, the congregation had grown to 80 members now. Someone had told Thomas the average congregation of a church in America was 70. The size of his congregation seemed more than enough to prove that Thomas was offering something people needed.

Church revivals are often energetic events, requiring enthusiastic preaching. Goals of a revival are to add new members to the church and to revive the spirits of the current members. T. D. Jakes enjoyed speaking at revivals; his animated style of delivering the gospel seemed particularly well suited for these events.

But he still had moments of despair. "I confess, I have cried huge salty tears," he said later in *Can You Stand to Be Blessed?* "I have felt the bitter pangs of rejection and criticism. I admit there were times that I rocked my worries to sleep in the middle of the night."

Things began looking up in 1983. Thomas started to preach over the radio on a weekly program, *The Master's Plan*, and his bass exhortations boomed and crackled across the West Virginia airwaves. That same year, he hosted a special conference for the members of his church and others who were interested, called "Back to the Bible," and he moved the Temple of Faith congregation's meeting place to a better facility in the nearby town of Smithers.

One weekend, a Pentecostal bishop named Sherman Watkins asked for T. D. Jakes's help in conducting a "revival." These religious meetings have become a tradition of the evangelical churches, especially the Pentecostals. One goal of a revival is to add new members to the church; another goal is to revive the spirit of the current membership. The preaching has to be intense—so intense that it would make smug churchgoers wake up. A revival is a real challenge to a preacher.

But Thomas seemed to do it very well. "I saw in him some potential," Bishop Watkins later told the *Dallas Morning News.* However, the bishop had been more impressed with Thomas than he admitted. He invited Thomas and his Temple of Faith congregation to join his own group of Pentecostal churches, the Higher Ground Always Abounding Assemblies. He offered Thomas the fancy title of "assistant presiding prelate." Another name given him was "Vice Bishop." During the next seven years, he would help Bishop Watkins preside over 200 churches.

In 1990 Thomas had an opportunity to start a new Temple of Faith Church in Charleston. The preacher jumped at the chance. Many members of his congregation lived closer to Charleston than

Smithers anyway, including one of his most faithful helpers, Stanley Miller, who had been with him since the Union Carbide days.

In Charleston, T. D.'s congregation soon numbered more than 100. And a wonderful thing happened. Some white faces peeked into the church timidly, not sure they were welcome. Thomas later told the *Dallas Morning News*, "They would come to my church and ask, 'Can white people come here?' I thought, 'What a crazy question.'" But then he thought about the invisible walls that divide American culture. Thomas wanted to knock down these walls. Soon he had a growing congregation that was almost one-third white.

His family was growing too. In 1987 the school-age twin sons had been joined by a baby daughter, Cora Brionne. She was calm and quiet from the moment she was born. Cora was creative but shy, and her quiet spirit spread tranquillity to everyone. She looked like her mother, and she guarded her thoughts, keeping her inmost being private.

Just eleven months later a second daughter, Sarah Dionne, arrived. Sarah was far different from her older sister. She screamed for whatever she wanted. Even as a baby, she used her temper to intimidate her family. She wasn't spoiled, but she was assertive and high-spirited.

Thomas was startled by the difference between his two daughters. He was certain this difference was no product of heredity or environment. Instead, he felt, these two different personalities had been given to his family by a God who loves diversity.

Thomas liked to say his children were God's way of sending him to school: he learned so much from them. When baby Cora got sick one time, another great truth was revealed to Thomas: his own parents' love for him. In the midst of his panic over baby Cora, he depended on his mother's support. The doctors had just told him that his baby would need to be

The many problems of women in his church community led T. D. Jakes to begin small counseling sessions. The Sunday sessions quickly grew, and Thomas realized that there were many women who needed relief from their personal pain. From these sessions grew a conference that he would one day entitle "Woman, Thou Art Loosed!"

hospitalized, and in a daze he drove to his mother's house. In his book *Daddy Loves His Girls*, he describes the conversation he had with his mother that day:

> I, with bulging eyes, asked my mother a question that neither of us will ever forget. 'Is this how you feel about me?' I blurted out. I never knew you could love anyone that much. To think that my own mother and father might feel that way about me, and I didn't even know it! Oh, I knew that they loved me. But I mean this desperate, insane, pulsing feeling that made me feel like the sun would never shine without my child and all the grass would cease to grow if she were not all right. I confess, I was amazed. . . . She replied softly, 'The way you feel about that child is the same way I feel about you.' Suddenly, I knew the secret that only parents

know. There is no word for it. You can only know it when you have your own child. It is the gift of love that God allows parents, or I should say good parents, to enjoy. . . . To think that I was loved like that and didn't know it!

This growing ability not only to feel but also to understand feelings was becoming a trademark of Thomas Dexter Jakes. Somehow he could sense and analyze emotions, especially in women. As a result he discovered that many women, especially African-American ones, were terribly hurt. This pain from the past was crippling. Their self-esteem was almost destroyed. In *The Lady, Her Lover and Her Lord*, Thomas describes these individuals as "broken woman," who wrap themselves in the only protection they can find: bitterness and anger.

Well, Thomas certainly knew about pain. He had every right to consider himself an expert. "My pain has been very diverse," he explained once in an interview in *Charisma*. "Everything from racism to poverty to brokenness, along with the struggle of day-to-day living." Hidden in his explanation was the immense hurt his father's death had caused him. But his father's death and Thomas's tangle of guilt and grief afterward had catapulted him into a wonderful calling.

In the same interview, he emphasized the irony he found in counseling the wounded. He had discovered, he said, that the things that hurt us the most can become the fuel that drives us toward our destiny. "It will either make you bitter or it will make you better," he said. "I wanted to be made better, not bitter."

Thomas used this wisdom as he counseled the hurting. The remedy he offered was not his own; he offered the power of Jesus. His counseling was built on the gospel. And as a pastor, of course he did not confine his counseling to African American women; he counseled males and females of all races and ages. Pain, as he had learned, is not prejudiced. It recognizes no gender and it includes all ages and ethnic groups. Thomas might have looked different from the people he counseled, but he could relate to them on the pain they had in common.

The large number of women in his congregation who sought counseling astounded him. Part of the reason for this number was that women were many likely than men to admit their feelings and seek help. But part of it was that there really were many women who were hurting. Thomas learned that he did not have enough hours in the day to meet privately with each woman who asked for counseling. After all, the size of his Temple of Faith congregation had doubled, to 200 members. So he started a Sunday group session for women. The class was immediately very popular.

"The problems were very similar, so I thought instead of counseling them one by one, maybe if I bring them all together I could tell them all the same thing at one time," he told the *Dallas Morning News*. "I just started teaching on it, and it ran over to the second class and the third and more people came every time. I'm not sure even to this day that I totally know how vast the need is."

In 1992 a pastor friend who lived in Pittsburgh asked T. D. Jakes to visit and counsel women there in a seminar. By now, Thomas had his presentation well organized, and he decided to give the program a name. He found it in a New Testament story in which Jesus performs a miracle for someone he spots in the crowd. The miracle is described in the 13th chapter of the Book of Luke:

> And, behold, there was a woman which had a spirit of infirmity eighteen years, and was bowed together, and could in no wise lift up herself. And when Jesus saw her, he called her to him, and said unto her, Woman, thou art loosed from thine infirmity. And he laid his hands on her: and immediately she was made straight, and glorified God.

So Thomas dubbed his seminar "Woman, Thou
Art Loosed." As the minister in Pittsburgh spread the
word about this seminar for women who were hurting, wounded, anguished, or abandoned, Pastor Jakes
prepared to try to help whoever showed up.

6

PROSPERITY

❦

WHEN THOMAS ARRIVED in Pittsburgh he was flabbergasted. Over 1,300 women had registered for his seminar "Woman, Thou Art Loosed." The program had to be moved to an enormous hotel ballroom.

Thomas found that many of the women were not even members of a church. They were coming out of desperation, hoping to ease their feelings of pain. Thomas was stunned. Yes, he had preached to his Temple of Faith congregation of 200 members. He had evangelized to bigger gatherings than that at revivals—but he had never spoken to 1,300 people. And he knew that many of these women who were not from a religious background would not respond to church rhetoric.

But Thomas felt that God would be with him. He knew his material, and he had never before wanted so desperately to pour healing waters on an audience. "Woman, thou art loosed from thine infirmity!" promised his seminar. And so he preached his heart out.

"Hidden inside of you is a great woman who can do great exploits in His name," he exhorted. "He wants that woman to be set free. He wants the potential within you to be unleashed so you can become the person you were created to be. . . .You have nothing to lose, and everything to gain. Jesus will straighten the crooked places in your heart and make

When Bishop T. D. Jakes arrived in Pittsburgh, he found that more than 1,300 women had signed up for his seminar "Woman, Thou Art Loosed." This response astounded him. Eventually, it would inspire him to formulate his seminar into a book of the same title.

you completely whole. When you allow Him access to every area of your life, you will never be the same broken person again."

After the conference, Thomas was deluged with praise. The pastor who had invited him was ecstatic. T. D. Jakes received a nice check for his work, money that he could use to provide for his family. But he decided instead to take a very daring step. Thomas took the funds to a book publisher in Shippensburg, Pennsylvania. Destiny Image specializes in Pentecostal books, but it is also a "subsidy" publisher. (That means the author pays Destiny Image to create and print the book. The author then tries to sell the product however he can.) Thomas told Destiny Image that he wanted to publish a book to provide the same counseling that his "Woman, Thou Art Loosed" conference did.

Destiny Image agreed, but the publisher did not like Thomas's title and instead suggested *Daughters of Liberty*. Jakes refused to change the title, for he believed it came right out of the Lord's mouth. He composed the book *Woman, Thou Art Loosed* with the same care he had composed sermons for 13 years.

For $15,000, Destiny Image printed 5,000 paperback copies. Jakes priced the book at about $10. The word was out among Pentecostals—and even among people who did not attend church—about T. D. Jakes' marvelous counseling for wounded women. As a result, Thomas sold the first printing in three weeks. The book continued to sell almost as fast at it could be printed. Soon, Jakes was a respected and nationally known counselor. As word about the book spread, *Woman, Thou Art Loosed* began selling at an incredible rate: 5,000 copies a week. Even after distribution costs, the profits from the book were staggering, perhaps as high as $1,000 per day!

Thomas only worked harder. He gave God all the credit for his success, and continued his counseling work. This time, he was ready to reach out to men.

Since publishing his first book in 1994, Thomas has been a prolific writer. He has sometimes been compared to C. S. Lewis (1898–1963), an English novelist and literary scholar who wrote many essays on Christian theological and moral problems, including The Problem of Pain *(1940),* The Screwtape Letters *(1942), and* Mere Christianity *(1952).*

He held a conference, titled "Manpower," in Detroit. The conference, designed to meet the special emotional needs of men, drew 2,500. Thomas gave the attendees a chance to express themselves. He even allowed them to cry.

He started a weekly television show called *Get Ready with T. D. Jakes* on both the Trinity Broadcasting Network and Black Entertainment Television. Thomas also poured the profits from his book into his ministry. He moved his congregation into a larger building, a renovated bank office in Cross Lanes,

Bill McCartney, the founder of the group Promise Keepers, addresses a rally. The Promise Keepers gatherings attract tens of thousands of Christian men who wish to rededicate themselves to their families and their churches. Bishop T. D. Jakes supported McCartney when his organization first became nationally known.

West Virginia, about 10 miles west of Charleston.

His congregation was growing rapidly. It now numbered in the hundreds. Meanwhile, he traveled to conduct conferences. He now had three in his repertoire: the Bible conference, "Manpower," and "Woman, Thou Art Loosed." He began to plan a fourth conference, one for wounded pastors and their wives, called "When Shepherds Bleed." He started T. D. Jakes Ministries, a nonprofit organization to administer the conferences and his television programs.

Thomas was pleased that his conferences were able to help so many people. "What's nice is that I

didn't study the Word to wow a crowd," he later commented. "I studied the Word to find healing, and when I found something that helped me, I got up and shared it. In fact, I opened my heart fearing that I would be laughed off a stage—only to find that people ran to me and said, 'me too.'

"So I'm not afraid to be different. I was probably the first male to climb up on a stage and minister to thousands upon thousands of women and acknowledge that they had a legitimate reason to be wounded."

During his spare time in 1994 and 1995, T. D. Jakes continued to write counseling books. He expressed himself in simple but moving words. And the words gushed forth as if he were a C. S. Lewis (the brilliant English scholar who wrote *Mere Christianity*). Over the years, Thomas had stored in his soul and mind hundreds of thousands of words for the hurting. Words, sentences, paragraphs, pages, chapters, entire books came forth in a torrent, seldom even needing to be revised. He told the *St. Louis Dispatch*, "I consider myself a conveyor belt of God's word."

With Destiny Image, Thomas authored two more books. *Can You Stand to Be Blessed?*, published in 1995, expresses a theme that Thomas now emphasizes regularly: the believer will succeed if he or she does not get discouraged. Thomas includes stories about his personal setbacks and sorrows to support his theme. His subtitle for the second book he published that year with Destiny Image, *Naked and Not Ashamed*, was "We've been afraid to reveal what God wants to heal." In this book, Thomas urges readers to peel off all their phoniness and reveal themselves to God, so they can heal. The ultimate example of this, he points out, is Jesus Christ, who was stripped and sacrificed, yet was glorious and unashamed.

Thomas also wrote two books for a second publisher, Pneuma Life, in Maryland. In *The Harvest* Thomas calls for "field workers" to save souls before it is too late. Time for the harvest might be running out, and this might be the last "crop" before Judgment Day. In *Help Me, I've Fallen*, Thomas explains how the fallen can recover. Naturally, the answer, he says, is the healing power of Jesus Christ.

Although the obligations of his ministry and his writing took much of his time, T. D. Jakes accepted another task: he became one of the most enthusiastic volunteers in Promise Keepers, an organization for men. Its goal is to commit men to keep their promises to God, to themselves, to their wives, to their families, to their friends, to their neighbors, and to their communities. Bill McCartney, a former football coach, had formulated the program. Although some groups opposed Promise Keepers, claiming that it excluded women, Thomas felt that the organization addressed a crying need: men must become responsible again. "I believe in what Bill McCartney is doing," Thomas told *Charisma*. "I believe he's making a major contribution to the body of Christ, and I'm proud to be part of it. He has flung high the welcome mat to all races to be part of the worship experience."

And despite the demands on his time, Thomas tried never to neglect his own family responsibilities as husband and father. In 1995, his third son, Thomas Dexter Jr., was born. Now he and Serita were blessed with five children: 14-year-old twins Jermaine and Jamar; Cora, 7; Sarah, 6; and baby Thomas. The feelings this child evoked in T. D. Jakes made writing yet another book—*Loose That Man and Let Him Go!*, for Albury Press, in Oklahoma—even easier. This book tells men how to recognize and hold on to their own identity.

McCartney loved the book. He told Amazon.com, the online bookstore, "Bishop Jakes presents a compelling argument for fatherhood that every man needs to read. Get the book into the hands of every guy you know! Read it in your home to your sons. You can't start too early. Send it to a friend or foe. God will use it to change lives!"

By 1996, *Woman, Thou Art Loosed* had sold over half a million copies. Thomas's other books had sold well too. He took the enormous profits from his book sales and spent them on his family. By his reckoning, they had waited long enough. For 15 years he and Serita had survived on a shoestring, and the twins had lived like paupers for 14 years. Thomas Jr., he decided, was not going to know poverty.

Thomas bought a huge 16-room house. He added a bowling alley and an indoor pool. He bought a Mercedes Benz car that cost $80,000, then purchased a second one. He knew people wanted to see him prosper. After all, wasn't prosperity one of his main messages? Trust God, he had always told his flock; it may be a long struggle, but you will prosper. He was certainly prospering. He began to wear tailored suits. He traveled first-class. He acquired jewelry.

Jakes was not so naive as to think no one would question his affluence. But his money did not come from his ministry. It came instead from the sales of his counseling books. He had worked long extra hours to get his books out, Thomas reasoned, so how could people question whether he had a right to collect the profits from this work?

But after he held one of his Bible conferences in Charleston, the local newspaper trashed him as a money-grubber. Thomas fought his anger. His conference had just brought more than 10,000 people into Charleston, and the visitors had spent several million dollars in the city. And now the newspaper attacked him! Where were his defenders? Where were all the people he had helped?

Thomas was surprised at the depth of his anger. The Charleston area was his home. He had grown up and risen from poverty there. Thomas thought about how his father had been excluded from skilled labor jobs, how his father had worked night and day cleaning toilets and emptying rubbish and mopping floors. He thought how hard his mother had worked to raise three children and teach school besides. He thought how in the early days of his marriage he had hauled water to Serita, who sat with twin babies in candlelight.

Now, the local newspaper was calling him an opportunistic money-grubber! Thomas became angrier and angrier. He held a press conference. He vented his anger on the press. He considered moving to another city.

Could Thomas leave his beloved Charleston? Jesus himself did not advocate endless patience with fools. "And whosoever shall not receive you, nor hear you, when ye depart thence, shake off the dust under your feet for a testimony against them," says Jesus in the Book of Mark.

That was exactly what Thomas would do. He would shake the dust off his feet and leave Charleston. But where would he go?

7

DALLAS MEGACHURCH

❦

EARLY IN 1996 Thomas learned that a television evangelist named W. V. Grant was being sent to jail for 16 months for failing to pay taxes on income. Grant was now forced to sell his Eagle's Nest Family Church in Dallas, Texas. Thomas's first reaction was to advise a pastor friend in that area to consider buying the facility. But after his disillusionment with Charleston, Thomas suddenly woke up one night with a start.

Later he told *Gospel Today,* "I really felt that it was a sovereign move of God. It wasn't an intellectual choice. On my own accord, I would not have chosen that particular city; not that I had any likes or dislikes—I just didn't know a lot about Dallas."

In April 1996, after he announced his plans to buy the facilities and move his own family and 50 of his Temple of Faith staff to Dallas, he was able to articulate God's reasons for the change in location. First, he felt that he had done all he could do in Charleston. Second, he was affiliated with the Trinity Broadcast Network (TBN), and a major part of TBN operates in Dallas. Third, the transportation network there allowed people to easily fly in for meetings and conferences. Besides all that, the Dallas–Fort Worth metroplex had twice the population of the entire state of West Virginia. The move made sense—but as always, Thomas gave God the credit for working

Bishop Jakes shows off the interior of The Potter's House facility in Dallas, Texas.

Evangelist W. V. Grant enters federal court for a sentencing hearing after his conviction for tax evasion. Hearing that Grant's large facility would be put up for sale, Thomas decided it was time to move from his hometown of Charleston, West Virginia, to Dallas, Texas.

through the circumstances.

With the help of a $1.9 million mortgage, T. D. Jakes Ministries acquired W. V. Grant's 28-acre site located in the Oak Cliff area of southwest Dallas. Although the acreage was near a freeway that tied Dallas to Fort Worth, the enormous barnlike church (with adjacent rooms to handle overflow crowds, it seated 5,000) was surrounded by open fields. Nearby were broadcast and print facilities. The entire package cost $3.2 million.

Thomas soon learned that the news of his move

had rippled out across the Dallas–Fort Worth area. Talk radio shows blared the worries of local pastors, who feared that T. D. Jakes Ministries would deplete their own flocks. Openly, however, most expressed their welcome. "As long as he keeps reaching people for Jesus, I have no problem with that," Pastor E. K. Bailey, vice president of the city's African American Pastors Coalition, told *Charisma*.

One of Thomas's friends, Clifford Frazier of Heartline Ministries, echoed the welcome as he talked to *Charisma*. "The more churches we have, the better. This focuses attention on Dallas. I think people will be won to Christ."

Certainly Thomas did not hide his candle under a basket. In the ultra-rich Lakewood area of Dallas, next to the mansion of billionaire H. L. Hunt, Thomas bought a $1.7 million mansion with eight bathrooms, five fireplaces, and a pool. Once again, he shrugged off criticism of his lavish lifestyle. Most African Americans agreed with him, feeling that Christian ministers did not need to take a vow of poverty.

Thomas felt he would be not only dishonest but also hypocritical if he hid the fact that he was making money as a businessman with his book royalties and speaking fees. After all, many of his sermons promised prosperity for those who persevered. He never promised instant riches, but he insisted that prosperity would eventually come for those who trusted God, endured tough times, and worked hard. He told the *Dallas Morning News*, "I don't think I've tried to flaunt it, nor have I tried to hide it. If it's not dishonest or illegal, it's irrelevant."

T. D. Jakes quickly threw his energy into renovating the huge church. He replaced the carpets and installed stained glass windows that showed praying hands on a backdrop of colorful wild birds playing in a green jungle paradise; his sanctuary was to appear like the Garden of Eden. Next, he added giant video screens above each side of the huge plexiglass altar.

T. D. Jakes was one of the consultants for the Robert Duvall film The Apostle, *which is about a Pentecostal preacher. Hoping to make the best film possible, Duvall spoke with and observed several Dallas-area preachers, using their insights and techniques in his own performance.*

Then, he strung video feeds to outlying rooms so that overflow crowds could watch his sermons. Thomas did not think small.

He exuded confidence and authority. Even though he had been in Dallas only a few weeks, he was included in a group of African-American ministers who met with movie star Robert Duvall. Duvall was making a movie about preachers. He would call it *The Apostle*, and he would star in it. He was meeting with the Dallas ministers to pick their brains for exceptional sermons and preaching techniques. Pentecostal preachers like T. D. Jakes especially attracted him, because their sermons were so fiery.

By the end of May 1996, Pastor Jakes began Sunday evening services at his church, which he had named The Potter's House. By July he added morning services. He also started trying to broaden the appeal of his church beyond African Americans. He sent out an appeal to Hispanics and whites, who made up 70 percent of Dallas's population. He welcomed them to

The Potter's House, emphasizing that it was not a "black" church.

He told *Charisma*, "If you ran a secular business that had no diversity in its leadership or ranks, you could be sued. Yet many churches have totally alienated other races. . . . It is an embarrassment to the body of Christ that even though segregated bathrooms and water fountains are gone, there are still 'black' and 'white' churches in this country."

As the church became more diverse, so did Thomas's own activities. Because of the popularity of his conference and book *Woman, Thou Art Loosed!*, in September 1996 Integrity Music recorded a live album during his "Woman Thou Art Loosed!" conference in the New Orleans superdome. Although professional recording was new for Pastor Jakes, for years he had interspersed preaching with singing. On the album he speaks, sings, leads prayers, and introduces guests. But he was especially excited to work with Shirley Caesar. Known as the Queen of Gospel, Shirley was an uncompromising gospel singer who had recorded more than 30 albums and won nine Grammy Awards, as well as numerous Dove Awards, which are given by the Gospel Music Association. Superstars like Whitney Houston and Mariah Carey were in awe of her, and so was Jakes. Hot sales of the album *Woman, Thou Art Loosed!—Songs of Healing and Restoration* seemed certain.

Bishop Jakes had long been praised for his ministry, and in 1996 he received two honors for his work. The magazine *Gospel Today* presented Thomas with its Gospel Heritage Award for Ministry, and he also received the Stellar Foundation's 1996 Excellence Award.

By the beginning of 1997 The Potter's House was in full swing, even offering a bilingual service for Hispanics. The appeal for diversity had made the congregation about 10 percent white and 4 percent Hispanic. Together, the church services were attracting about 10,000 participants weekly. Serita was now the human resources director of The Potter's House, which had a staff of 200 people. So many drove to the church services that off-duty policemen had to be hired to direct traffic in the parking lot. Six cameras filmed each sermon. From those six films a videocassette was made. The video sold for $20. An audiocassette sold for $5. Thousands of tapes were sold every week.

The pastor did not hesitate to influence people to be generous to The Potter's House. He would remind visitors to the church, "You take care of God's business and He'll take care of you." Before the collection plates were passed, he would ask those who tithe (that is, give 10 percent of their income) to wave their white envelopes in the air. Then he invited them to bring their envelopes directly to the altar. They sang and waved their envelopes as they danced down the aisles. After that powerful display, the collection plates were passed.

Thomas wrote more books, making publishers bid on them. Creation House published *Help! I'm Raising My Children Alone* and *Daddy Loves His Girls*. Pneuma Life published three books: *Why? Because You Are Anointed*, *Anointing Fall on Me*, and *Water in the Wilderness*. Yet another book, *T. D. Jakes Speaks to Women*, was handled by Albury Press. Thousands of his books were being sold every day.

By July The Potter's House was drawing 13,000 people a week, and Thomas burned the $1.9 million mortgage. In just one year he had paid it off. The amount of money flowing into The Potter's House and T. D. Jakes Ministries attracted the attention of Ole Anthony of the Trinity Foundation. The foundation was a watchdog group that monitored activities of churches. Anthony had sounded the alarms that brought down the ministries of W. V. Grant and Robert Tilton. But Ole Anthony finally had to admit he could find no evidence whatever of any improper

financial dealings in the T. D. Jakes Ministries.

Unruffled by criticism about his affluent lifestyle, Thomas unloosed another barrage of books in 1997, again using different publishers. He used TDK Publishers for the first time with *I Choose to Forgive*. Pneuma Life published both *When Shepherds Bleed* and *A Fresh Glimpse of the Dove*. Albury Press published three: *So You Call Yourself a Man?*, *T. D. Jakes Speaks to Men*, and *Lay Aside the Weight*. The latter book was a major departure for Thomas. It dealt with the fact that the men in his family were disposed to become grossly overweight, causing high blood pressure and ultimately kidney failure.

Serita Jakes receives flowers from Wanda Cunningham, CEO and founder of Women of the Southern Region, as T. D. Jakes looks on. Serita is a very active partner in Bishop Jakes's ministry, working as the human resources director of Potter's House and overseeing the church's staff of 200.

Bishop Jakes was excited to work with award-winning Gospel singer Shirley Caesar on the album Woman, Thou Art Loosed!—Songs of Healing and Restoration. *Caesar is shown here standing to the left of Whitney Houston's mother, Cissy Houston, at the 1997 Grammy Awards ceremony.*

In the book Thomas explains that somehow he had ignored the fact that during the past 17 years his own size 40 pants had ballooned to their current size 56! His suit coat was a tent. He weighed 338 pounds! Suddenly he had realized he was overworked, overweight, and bloated—just like his father had been. He could be suffering severe kidney damage. He saw a doctor, then learned proper diet from a nutritionist. With the power of Christ, he peeled off 110 pounds, dropping to 228. Wife Serita also joined in this new battle; she lost 41 pounds. Thomas felt so strongly about his new healthy lifestyle that he wrote *Lay Aside the Weight* to help people with similar weight problems.

Another new development occurred in his writing career in 1997. This evolved as a result of his growing celebrity. The large publishing house G. P. Putnam & Son signed Thomas to a two-book deal for $1.8 million. Implied in the deal was that Putnam would run an enormous publicity campaign to sell the books. If Thomas was still unknown to many Americans, that seemed likely to change.

8

BLESSED FUTURE

❦

W HEN MOTHER TERESA passed away in Cal-
cutta, India, on September 5, 1997, reporters sought
T. D. Jakes as the spokesman to articulate the sympa-
thies of the African-American community. This was
a sign of his growing respect and influence as a religious leader. He told the *Evangelical Press Association*,
"The world has lost a great soldier of the faith and a
matriarch of mercy. We join the rest of the world in
enveloping those closest to her in prayer and wince in
pain from the tremendous loss that we feel."

Another sign of the respect for Bishop T. D. Jakes
was his invitation to attend a prayer breakfast at the
White House with other important religious leaders
in September 1998.

Since his election in 1992, President Bill Clinton
had been dogged by various scandals. The day before
the prayer breakfast, the House of Representatives
had released a report by Kenneth Starr, the independent prosecutor who was investigating potential
wrongdoing in the White House, that revealed that
Clinton, a married man, had engaged in an affair with
a young White House intern, then lied about their
relationship while under oath. During this meeting,
Clinton asked the religious leaders for forgiveness.

Although Bishop Jakes was willing to forgive the
president, he later described the scandal as a "lost
opportunity [for the religious community] to lay

*Texas governor George W.
Bush shakes hands with
Bishop Jakes at the March
1998 dedication ceremony for
the minister's City of Refuge
project.*

down a template for men who are trapped. This is step-by-step-by-step how you come out of it."

"[President Clinton] is very typical of a high-powered, midlife individual, who no doubt is facing some form of midlife crisis, in a position of being stressed out over work, admired by young girls and married to a woman who's also involved in a lot of work," the Bishop said in a later sermon. "I thought his repentance was necessary because his actions were deplorable, inappropriate and appalling. To acknowledge that was the first step, to repent was the second step, and to open up to counseling was the third step. But all of that got washed away in the political meanderings, and that was tragic."

When the four Dallas Cowboys were baptized in November 1997, it seemed to many that 40-year-old T. D. Jakes had just popped up out of nowhere. Of course, this was not true. The Potter's House was one of the fastest growing churches in the nation. Thomas held five services, on Saturday, Sunday, and Wednesday, for a congregation of 17,000 that overwhelmed the capacity of The Potter's House. A man of many words, he had preached live, on television, and over the radio. He had conducted conferences all over the nation. He had written over a dozen books on Christian counseling, with sales in the millions. The baptism of the Cowboys just brought him greater national attention.

Old friend Stanley Miller, who had remained at the Temple of Faith back in the Charleston area as senior pastor, told *Charisma*, "Anointed is an understatement. That's one of the highest accolades you can give a person. But, somehow, for him that doesn't say it all." In the same article, Bishop Sherman Watkins marveled, "He's pregnant with God's purpose."

In spite of this multitude of accomplishments, Thomas revealed a staggering new project in March 1998: his plan for the City of Refuge, which was called Project 2000. Thomas used the Old Testament

Emmitt Smith is baptized by Bishop T. D. Jakes at the Potter's House church in Dallas. The move from Charleston to a larger facility in one of the biggest metropolitan areas of the country enabled Jakes's ministry to grow rapidly.

phrase "city of refuge" to name a place that would offer sanctuary for the troubled. Texas governor George W. Bush and Dallas mayor Ron Kirk joined Thomas at The Potter's House, where they all symbolically added some clay to a pot being made on a potter's wheel.

Cheered by 5,000 onlookers, T. D. Jakes said, "God delights in doing what the State cannot. In the name of Christ, the City of Refuge will show that statistics [of crime and poverty] change when hearts change." He went on to say, "Every one of these programs [offered by the City of Refuge] represents a human need and a God-filled response. The bedrock of the entire program is the relationship between people so weary they can only say 'I can't,' and people who respond with a committed, 'I care.'"

Governor Bush endorsed Thomas's plan. Mayor Kirk, who had attended The Potter House's "Seed & Feed" of 1,500 homeless the previous Thanksgiving, praised Thomas's ministry. They appreciated all he was doing to make a difference in Dallas.

In the spring of 1999, the enormous 10-year Project 2000 undertaking began. The church purchased 231 acres adjacent to The Potter's House for $3.5 million. The scope of Thomas's new city for the downtrodden was breathtaking. At its center would be the enormous GEAR (Generation's Exercising, Academics, and Restoration) building. It would house classrooms and study halls where people could take literacy courses, study for a General Equivalency Diploma (GED; the equivalent of a high school diploma), receive employment training, and work in computer labs.

Thomas wanted to treat the whole person. So naturally the GEAR building also had state-of-the-art gyms, a swimming pool, a weight room, locker rooms, a 1000-seat cafeteria, and an auditorium.

Other buildings in Project 2000 would include a preschool through high school complex; a retirement center; women's care center; executive retreat for business and religious leaders; a performing arts facility; a small business incubator; and a community auditorium. Thomas trumpeted the news that the City of Refuge—like The Potter's House—was dedicated to mending and reshaping broken lives through the love of Jesus Christ.

In April 1998 Thomas continued his publicity onslaught for Project 2000 at the Dallas Convention Center, where he was hosting a Bible conference. As 10,000 attendees cheered, Dallas Cowboy Deion

T. D. Jakes's most famous convert, Deion Sanders, has maintained his commitment to Christ. In 1998 he donated $1 million to the Bishop's City of Refuge project.

Sanders wrote a $1 million check for Project 2000. Sanders had not slid back to his old ways, as many cynics had predicted. He was still committed to Christ. He had not let his success lure him away from his new lifestyle.

Cowboy star Emmitt Smith had remained staunch in his faith too. In December 1998 Emmitt was highly visible at The Potter's House, handing out 26-pound boxes of canned vegetables, cereal, rice, pasta, crackers, beverages, and baby food to needy families in the church's "Feed the Children" cam-

With his sound advice, fiery preaching style, and millions of followers, Bishop T. D. Jakes seems poised to become the evangelical giant of the new millenium.

paign. Emmitt paid for much of the food himself. Many a child glowed with happiness after personally receiving help from the football star.

Thomas still carried out all his other activities. He regularly conducted his four conferences: the Bible conference, his conference for women, "Manpower," and "When Shepherds Bleed." In mid-1998 he demonstrated his colossal drawing power when his "Woman, Thou Art Loosed!" conference drew 52,000 people in Atlanta. This almost coincided with the release of his long-awaited book from Putnam.

The new book and its author were praised by *Publishers Weekly*, which wrote, "Bishop T. D. Jakes— a writing, lecturing and preaching legend within evangelical Protestant Christian circles—is poised to conquer the general trade with *The Lady, Her Lover and Her Lord*. . . . [Putnam's] director of religious publishing [calls] Jakes 'a black Billy Graham with the impact of Martin Luther King.' . . . [Putnam's director says,] 'This book, like all of his books, is Bible-based and uses the scriptures. His message is for the churched and the unchurched—a message of healing for people who are hurting.'" Sales of the hardcover book were phenomenal, quickly vaulting past 500,000.

Thomas was developing a presence in music as well. The album *Woman, Thou Art Loosed!—Songs of Healing and Restoration* had been nominated for both Grammy and Dove Awards. In 1998 he received a contract to record an album for PolyGramUS. When *Sacred Love Songs* was released, some persons in the music industry called the album "gospel-pop" in an attempt to categorize a project that didn't fit neatly into any existing music category, but Thomas described the record as "sacred music for married couples." He should have known, for he wrote the words to all the songs, and his deep bass voice purred over gospel vocals of professional singers. But that was not all. Thomas also recorded another album for Integrity Music: *T. D. Jakes and The Potter's House Choir Live at The Potter's House*. The album was so well done that it hit the Billboard R&B music chart.

Like Billy Graham, Thomas never hesitated to open doors for people in need. In 1998 he was invited by WorldReach to help spread the Word through central Africa. WorldReach already reached one million Nigerians in west Africa with Christian radio and television programs. Central Africa was in turmoil with ethnic wars so horrific they rivaled the Holocaust of World War II. How could Thomas refuse to help?

Bishop Jakes and The Potter's House have also been very active in helping prison inmates through The Potter's House New Creation Ministry, which provides religious, educational, and rehabilitational broadcast programs. And because not all states' prison systems have the capability to receive satellite broadcasts, The Potter's House also started a national Adopt-A-Prison campaign to organize and support the donation of satellite equipment to prisons. The first donations of equipment came in Louisiana, where the state's 25 adult and juvenile correctional facilities began receiving The Potter's House programming in April and May of 1999 over satellite dishes that had been paid for by Louisiana churches, organizations, and individuals. At the same time, The Potter's House was trying to negotiate similar programs with corrections officials in New York, Ohio, Georgia, and Mississippi.

"The most confining prison is the one of lost opportunity, and we have prisons full of lost opportunity," said Jakes. "More than a million lives can be restored by bringing in God and providing education, life skills, and practical ways to help the incarcerated break out of their internal prisons and freely live out spiritual teachings."

By mid-1999, The Potter's House was working with more than 540 adult correctional facilities in the United States, Canada, and Japan. Bishop Jakes's message reached more than 500,000 inmates in 1998, said George Fitzgerald, the director of New Creation Ministry. Fitzgerald offered himself as an example of the good that religious and educational programming can do in prisons. A convicted felon, he spent 13 years in prison before earning an associate degree in Juvenile Corrections and becoming involved in prison ministry. "I'm living proof that people can change if provided the resources and given the opportunity," he said.

In November 1998 Thomas announced plans for a new Potter's House. His enormous congregation was increasing at the rate of 500 new members every month. Construction of an 8,400-seat stopgap facility—next to the "old" Potter's House—began in February 1999. Eventually the ministry would build a 14,000-seat sanctuary. The new Potter's House would cost $17 million.

If Thomas said it was going to happen, it would happen. He was building T. D. Jakes Ministries into an evangelical empire. He was being compared more and more often to Billy Graham, the highly respected evangelist who had built a gigantic evangelical empire that spanned more than 50 years. In fact, in August 1999 Thomas's "Woman, Thou Art Loosed!" conference in Atlanta's Georgia Dome drew 85,000 people, breaking a single-day attendance record held by Reverend Graham.

T. D. Jakes has said that he never thought his message would reach so many people. But each year hundreds of thousands come to his church services, tune in to his radio and television broadcasts, read his books, or attend his conferences. "My assignment," he notes in an Integrity Music profile, "is to open the doors of the church to hurting people and to redefine what the church was meant to be in our society. The church has become stereotyped as a spiritual club for elitists and yuppies who portray themselves as persons who have arrived. I think the church was meant to be a hospital for hurting people—people who have not arrived, which is just about all of us whether we want to admit it or not."

As Billy Graham was the evangelical giant of the 20th century, Thomas seems destined to be the evangelical giant of the 21st century. He has come a long way from his poor West Virginia roots. The backwoods boy who was broken by sorrow and hardship now uses his miraculous resources to spread a message of healing and plenty.

CHRONOLOGY

1957   Born Thomas Dexter Jakes on June 9 near Charleston, West Virginia, the third and last child of Odith and Ernest Jakes

1967   Becomes his father's caretaker, as Ernest, with failing kidneys, must have ever increasing care at home

1973   When his father dies, finds relief only in Pentecostal church and is seized by a craving to read the Bible and preach

1974   Discouraged from preaching by his inexperience and a speech impediment, enrolls as a psychology major at West Virginia State College

1976   Leaves college and drifts around the Charleston area as a poor, itinerant preacher

1980   Becomes pastor at Temple of Faith in Montgomery, West Virginia; marries Serita Jamison

1983   Begins broadcasting weekly radio program *The Master's Plan* and holds "Back to the Bible" conference; becomes vice bishop of 200 Pentecostal churches known as the Higher Ground Always Abounding Assemblies

1990   Starts the Temple of Faith Church in Charleston, West Virginia

1992–93   Counseling seminar for women grows from regional conference to best-selling book, *Woman, Thou Art Loosed!*; hosts weekly television show *Get Ready with T. D. Jakes* and creates nonprofit organization T. D. Jakes Ministries

1994–95   Writes several more successful counseling books; adds counseling conferences for men and pastors

1996   Moves to Dallas to launch "megachurch" Potter's House

1997   Baptizes four Dallas Cowboys, solidifying his national reputation, and continues writing several more books

1998   Launches the 232-acre City of Refuge, a vast complex in Dallas, to help the hurting, and a new 14,000-seat Potter's House; album *Woman, Thou Art Loosed!— Songs of Healing and Restoration* nominated for Grammy and Dove Awards

APPENDIX: The Rise of Pentecostalism

The Pentecostal Church was born at the turn of the twentieth century on Azusa Street in Los Angeles, California. That's where a two-year revival began that brought attention to the Pentecostal denomination of Christianity. The Azusa Street revival was the beginning of a religious movement that would see its membership swell to approximately 50 million by 1980.

Seen by many as a fringe religion due to its members' belief in speaking in tongues —where God speaks through an individual in a language unknown to man—Pentecostals basically subscribe to traditional Christian doctrines. Their belief in speaking in tongues sets them apart. They refer to it as "Baptism in the Holy Spirit."

While the majority of those in American society are skeptical of the idea of speaking in tongues, Pentecostals claim few understand it. At least one article on the subject claims that speaking in tongues is mentioned 35 times in the Bible. The article suggests that speaking in tongues edifies a person, or charges him up spiritually. Pentacostals often quote from the Bible to help demonstrate the worth of speaking in tongues. "For he that speaketh in an unknown tongue speaketh not unto men, but unto God: for no man understandeth *him*; howbeit in the spirit he speaketh mysteries" (1 Corinthians 14:2).

In 1898, Charles Fox Parham, an independent preacher in Topeka, Kansas, began teaching scripture in his home to a small group of students. His teachings included justification by sanctification, divine healing, the pre-millennium Second Coming of Christ, and intense study of scriptural evidence of receiving the Holy Spirit by speaking in tongues. The teachings are based on the account of the Pentecost—the day Christ appeared to the Apostles after his crucifixion—in which the Holy Spirit descended on the early Christians with many signs and wonders, including speaking in tongues.

Agnes Ozman, one of Parham's students, was baptized in the Holy Spirit and was one of the first to actually begin to speak in tongues. Parham and others soon had the experience. The movement began to grow and Parham eventually moved his school to Houston, Texas. Despite segregation laws, a Southern black preacher named William Joseph Seymour joined Parham's classes.

By 1906, Seymour had become the central figure of the movement. He was invited to preach in a black Nazarene church in Los Angeles. In his very first sermon he preached about speaking in tongues. Because he had never actually spoken in tongues, Seymour was locked out of the Nazarene church for preaching about it.

Despite this he continued to spread the Pentecostal beliefs from his home. His home prayer meetings became so large he soon sought out a new location. Finally, an abandoned building on Azusa Street became the home of Seymour's services.

For over two years, services were held three times a day. When the revival finally ended, hundreds of evangelists and missionaries left Asuza to begin spreading the Word. The Pentecostal beliefs were spread across the United States and the world. The early converts to the religious sect consisted primarily of poor farmers and mill hands. Also populating the ranks of the Pentecostals were poor rural-to-urban migrants as well as foreign-born immigrants. While there were other Pentecostal preachers at the time, Seymour was clearly the spark of the Azusa revival.

The religion appealed to many of the disenfranchised of the early 20th century society. Pentecostals do not discriminate by gender or race, and they are led by numerous black and female ministers. Other prominent members of the early Pentecostal movement included Alma White, head of the Pillar of Fire church in Denver; Manie Ferguson, who operated and founded the Peniel Mission in Los Angeles; and Florence Crawford, the editor of *The Apostolic Faith*.

As successful as the religion may have appeared early on, that success didn't last long. A major split among Pente-

costals in the 1920s over doctrinal and sociological issues splintered the group into three sections. This internal conflict kept the groups isolated from other Christians, furthering the impression of the religion as being on the fringe.

The charismatic career of Aimee Semple McPherson (pictured above), which began in the 1920s, brought new recruits and national publicity to the group. In 1921, McPherson became the first woman in history to preach a sermon over the airwaves. Her weekly broadcast made her one of the most influential preachers in the nation, reaching more than 5,300 people. The suffering caused by the Great Depression made even more people to turn to McPherson and Pentecostalism. McPherson also introduced jazz music into the church and popularized the use of sermons illustrated and dramatized through stage plays. Her popularity lasted into the 1940s, despite controversy over her allegedly staging her own kidnapping and having an affair with a married man.

By the 1940s much of the Pentecostal membership was in the middle-class and the group needed a new direction. Oral Roberts and other healing evangelists—preachers who claim God can heal people through them if the sick have enough faith—created a new wave of Pentecostalism nationally and around the world. In the late 1950s another movement, the Charismatic, or neo-Pentecostals, failed to reach large numbers. The Charismatics established Pentecostal groups within Protestant denominations and the Roman Catholic Church, but never persuaded these groups to leave their original church. Finally, by the late 1970s the thrust of Pentecostalism shifted to Latin America and Africa.

Today Pentecostalism is a worldwide movement that is very much alive in the United States. The religious sect claims adherents in Pentecostal denominations, independent churches, and charismatic prayer groups in mainstream Protestant denominations and the Roman Catholic Church. Some of the largest Pentecostal denominations in the United States include Assemblies of God, the Church of God in Christ, the Church of God, the Pentecostal Holiness Church, and the United Pentecostal.

APPENDIX: The Emergence of the Megachurch

In simple terms, a megachurch is any church with a congregation of 1,000 or more members. But there is more to these churches than the mere numbers of their congregants. The mission of the megachurch is to meet the needs of the people it serves—and not just their spiritual needs. It is not uncommon for megachurches to have state-of-the-art health club facilities, along with a host of services such as sports and athletic leagues, child and elder care, and parenting and financial counseling classes.

What makes the megachurch appealing to some people is that it gives individuals a sense of community. With the rapid population growth of America's major cities and suburban areas, some people feel isolated and unconnected. The successful megachurches have identified these feelings and developed services and programs that attempt to meet the

needs of their members. These programs help bring people with similar interests together, creating smaller groups within the larger whole, and giving many individuals a sense of belonging. Not neglecting the spiritual, megachurches present the biblical message in a contemporary fashion, attempting to express it in a format that is relevant to everyday life. Many megachurches have exchanged organ music and choirs for guitars, drums, and pop-style music forms. Even the physical structure of the megachurch is an expression of its mission. The whitewashed clapboard church with pointed steeple spire has been replaced with a more multipurpose facility, able to accommodate a basketball tournament on Saturday night and worship services the following Sunday morning.

While outwardly these megachurches may seem unusual, they attempt to serve a purpose not unlike their counterparts did nearly a century ago. In America's early history, the church served as a place to express one's spirituality as well as a social gathering place. The church was the focal point of one's life. In church people were married, children were baptized, the dead were mourned. The church helped people deal with the joys and hardships of everyday life. Shared experiences gave these early Americans a sense of belonging and community.

Today's megachurches are providing a similar purpose. By providing unique programs and services, the megachurch has become the vehicle by which a large number of people experience a sense of belonging. The methods and appearances of the two kinds of churches may be different, but peoples' needs are the same, making the megachurch not so different from its early American prototype.

BOOKS BY T. D. JAKES

——— ❧ ———

Woman, Thou Art Loosed! Shippensburg, Pa.: Destiny Image, 1994

Can You Stand to Be Blessed? Shippensburg, Pa.: Destiny Image, 1995

Help Me, I've Fallen. Lanham, Md.: Pneuma Life, 1995

The Harvest. Lanham, Md.: Pneuma Life, 1995

Naked and Not Ashamed. Shippensburg, Pa.: Destiny Image, 1995

Loose That Man and Let Him Go! Tulsa, Okla.: Albury Press, 1996

Daddy Loves His Girls. Orlando, Fla.: Creation House, 1996

Water in the Wilderness. Lanham, Md.: Pneuma Life, 1996

Why? Because You Are Anointed. Lanham, Md.: Pneuma Life, 1996

T. D. Jakes Speaks to Women. Tulsa, Okla.: Albury Press, 1996

Help, I'm Raising My Children Alone. Orlando, Fla.: Creation House, 1996

Anointing Fall on Me. Lanham, Md.: Pneuma Life, 1997

A Fresh Glimpse of the Dove. Lanham, Md.: Pneuma Life, 1997

When Shepherds Bleed. Lanham, Md.: Pneuma Life, 1997

T. D. Jakes Speaks to Men. Tulsa, Okla.: Albury Press, 1997

I Choose to Forgive. Dallas: TDK Publishing, 1997

So You Call Yourself a Man? Tulsa, Okla.: Albury Press, 1997

Lay Aside the Weight. Tulsa, Okla.: Albury Press, 1997

The Lady, Her Lover, and Her Lord. New York: G. P. Putnam and Sons, 1998

FURTHER READING

Bartleman, Frank. *Azusa Street*. New York: Anchor reprint, 1997.

Brooks, Philip. *The Joy of Preaching*. Grand Rapids, Mich.: Kregel Publications, 1989.

Clemmons Ithiel. *Bishop C. H. Mason and the Roots of the Church of God in Christ*. Lanham, Md.: Pneuma Life Publishing, 1997.

Gilmore, Gayraud S. *Black Religion and Black Radicalism: An Interpretation of the Religious History of African Americans*. Maryknoll, N.Y.: Orbis Books, 1998.

Jakes, T. D. *Can You Stand to Be Blessed?* Shippensburg, Pa.: Destiny Image Publishers, 1995.

———. *Daddy Loves His Girls*. Orlando, Fla.: Creation House, 1996.

———. *Help! I'm Raising My Children Alone*. Orlando, Fla.: Creation House, 1996.

Sanders, Deion. *Power, Money and Sex*. Nashville, Tenn.: Word Publishing, 1998.

Synan, Vincent. *The Holiness-Pentecostal Tradition*. Grand Rapids, Mich.: William B. Eerdmans Publishing, 1997.

Wellman, Sam. *Billy Graham: The Great Evangelist*. Uhrichsville, Ohio: Barbour and Company, 1996.

INDEX

PICTURE CREDITS

SAM WELLMAN lives in Kansas. He has degrees from colleges in the Midwest and the Ivy League. He has written a number of biographies for both adults and younger readers. His books are about various notable people, people as diverse as Michelle Kwan, George Washington Carver, Mother Teresa, and Billy Graham.

NATHAN IRVIN HUGGINS, one of America's leading scholars in the field of black studies, helped select the titles for the BLACK AMERICANS OF ACHIEVEMENT series, for which he also served as senior consulting editor. He was the W. E. B. DuBois Professor of History and Afro-American Studies at Harvard University and the director of the W. E. B. DuBois Institute for Afro-American Research at Harvard. He received his doctorate from Harvard in 1962 and returned there as professor in 1980 after teaching at Columbia University, the University of Massachusetts, Lake Forest College, and the California State University, Long Beach. He was the author of four books and dozens of articles, including *Black Odyssey: The Afro-American Ordeal in Slavery*, *The Harlem Renaissance*, and *Slave and Citizen: The Life of Frederick Douglass*, and was associated with the Children's Television Workshop, National Public Radio, the Boston Athenaeum, the Museum of Afro-American History, the Howard Thurman Educational Trust, and Upward Bound. Professor Huggins died in 1989, at the age of 62, in Cambridge, Massachusetts.